Standing Tall

Willie Long
And the Mare Island
Original 21ers

A Legacy of Courage, Activism,
and Social Justice

Jake Sloan

ISBN-13: 978-1-942860-02-0

Published by:
WISR Press of the Western Institute for Social Research, Berkeley, CA
In association with
The African American Development Institute, Richmond, CA

DEDICATION

Dedicated to all the 21ers and their families

Contents

Foreword

In writing and subsequently publishing *Standing Tall: Willie Long And The Mare Island Original 21ers*, author Jake Sloan assumed literary leadership in telling the story of the quest for economic and social justice for African American workers who were employed by the federal government at Mare Island Naval Shipyard in the 1960s. His body of work interrogates the concepts of equality and democracy that are embodied in the ethos of the United States and expands the scope of civil rights scholarship. The book stands as a testament to sacrifice, the value and imperative of organization, solidarity and risk associated with speaking up and speaking out. Indeed, those who blaze new trails must be willing to face the headwinds. More so than the monument on Mare Island that pays tribute to the original 21ers, the book acknowledges the courage and resolve that is indicative of the struggle for justice for African American people that dates back to the Trans-Atlantic Slave Trade. The work is essential for the realization that there are those who attempt to tell the story of African American people but what they produce is biased, grossly distorted, triumphalism/revisionist and tantamount to fomented misconceptions. In general, the story of working people who fought for their humanity and self-respect is untold. The mental labor that Jake Sloan engaged in is a tribute to the original 21ers who were central figures in local Black Power labor politics.

Standing Tall: Willie Long And The Mare Island Original 21ers makes a contribution to the history of this country from the standpoint of telling a story that is not well-known, but in its essence bears witness to standing up for one's rights, the critical importance of leadership, using the system of jurisprudence as a tool and the need to have a cogent agenda in the quest for equality. The story of the original 21ers took place in the larger context of a national movement for civil rights and social justice. As part of the war industry, the more than 1,000 African American workers on Mare Island Naval Shipyard were confronted with racial discrimination in working conditions, unequal pay, hiring, training and advancement while the federal government and larger society spewed platitudes about democracy, liberty and equality manifesting a glaring contradiction. The small number of African Americans workers who signed the racial discrimination complaint were compelled to confront the very government that was supposed to defend their rights and freedoms while they were also confronted with resistance among the ranks of African American workers themselves. The book confirms that freedom is not free and represents substantiation of the value of collective action as opposed to individualism.

Across the country, there are unmarked graves of unsung heroes and heroines who represent countless acts of resistance which stand as testaments to the enduring struggle of African American people in the struggle for equality, democracy and economic justice. *Standing Tall: The Mare Island Original 21ers* as a monument that brings to light a virtually unknown group of men who made history by standing up for what was right and just.

Leonard McNeil is a former council member and mayor in the city of San Pablo, California, a retired political science professor at Contra Costa College, and a retired union iron worker in Local #378.

Preface: Why the Story?

That persistent continuity of the human experience is why studying history remains about the only way to understand who we were, are, and will be.
---Victor David Hanson

In 1961, there were an estimated one thousand plus African Americans working at Mare Island Naval Shipyard (hereinafter also referred to as Mare Island or The Shipyard) in Vallejo, California, with the great majority of them being men. For decades, they had suffered under organized, systematic, and, sometimes, unconscious discriminatory working conditions in hiring, training, promotions, and equal pay opportunities. In many ways, the working conditions for those in the production shops were better than those found in the private sector for similar work, especially in the building trades. However, increasingly, for at least the three decades preceding 1960, there had been growing dissatisfaction with the status quo among a small but growing group of the African American workers, especially among those working in the "skill" trades. In 1961, a relatively small group of the African American workers, constituting less than 5% of its total number employed at Mare Island, led by Willie Long, decided to organize and file a complaint of discrimination with the Federal Government. Notwithstanding resistance and foot-dragging from the leadership in Washington, at Mare Island, and eventual internal strife within the group's leadership, that action helped to bring about slow but measurable long-term change at The Shipyard, as well as at other federal installations in the area and beyond.

It will be shown that, over time, the action of filing the complaint would result in more equality in the hiring, placement, training, promotions and pay for African Americans at Mare Island and beyond, but sometimes with mixed results, especially at the human and personal levels. Moreover, and maybe more importantly, in the long run, the action, and related subsequent events, brought about a building of a brotherhood, a great sense of pride among the men involved--a pride that would live on long after Mare Island closed in 1996. That story is worth telling, and, in telling it, to the best of my ability, I will also reflect upon some of the larger issues that can be taken from it. In some ways, as I will show, the story is personal.

I felt that I simply had to tell the story, because it is important, for the men involved, for their immediate families and descendants, and for history, especially for the history of African Americans, a history which is still, in too many cases, often inadequately captured and told, especially at the level of "everyday people."

***

Beginning in what I remember as mid-to-late 1960 or early 1961, I started to participate in what would become a small, but I think an important part of the movement towards equal employment, training, promotional and equitable pay policies at Mare Island and at other federal installations in the San Francisco/Oakland Bay Area. At that time, I joined a group of African American men who were organizing to address the long-standing problems. I became part of what would, eventually, become known as The Original 21ers, a group of 25 men who went on to file a complaint with the Federal Government, in formal protest against discrimination at Mare Island, in November of that year.[1]

At the time, in 1961, it was neither my destiny nor my desire to be a leader in either the organization of the 21ers or in the later direction of the group. This was true, although I was either the third or fifth man to sign the complaint, depending on the order of how the document was signed, which is no longer possible to determine. In any case, at best, I was just a minor foot soldier in the effort, albeit committed to the cause. In no way was I prepared to be more. However, I have come to believe that it was and is my destiny, and certainly is my desire, to help assure that history will recognize the leaders and the importance of all the 21ers, although, at the time, I did not know and, indeed, could not have known, that it was my destiny.

At the time, I had no preparation for the task of writing the story, in any sense. I was neither what could be considered an intellectual nor a scholar. In fact, I was not even a decent student. I had dropped out of high school with a

10th grade education on paper and, probably, a 6th grade education in reality, when I had first joined the Army at the age of 15, in 1956, just a few, short years before the organization of what would become the 21ers. I only began to recognize my destiny many years later, around 1980. The reality is that, in 1961, I never could have even thought of writing a paper or a book about the events that evolved, even if I had had the capacity to do such writing, which I most decidedly did not. Indeed, in all probability, neither the leaders of the 21ers nor others saw the historical importance of what they were doing at the time. I certainly did not. For us, it was mainly important not from a larger, historical perspective, but only in the immediate sense of addressing the injustices that we, and other African Americans working with us, were experiencing. That is, it was immediately important to us for the potential of fair access to training, promotions and pay increases, not to mention increased respect, and for future opportunities for those African Americans who would come after us.

In a way, it is ironic that I would be the one to write the history of these important events, because I was, by far, the one who played the least important role in either the organizational formation or the implementation of its objectives. I was, however, deeply committed to the cause and, ultimately, probably became the best qualified to write the story, based on my later academic training in history, and because of my direct participation in some of the events, at least in the beginning. The one thing that I knew then and I know now, beyond a doubt, is that the other men involved, especially the leaders, were, and remain, in my mind, some of the greatest men that I have known or worked with, bar none. They influenced me in many ways. For example, I do not think I would have ever given serious thought to getting a higher education without the influence of some of the men involved, especially that of Charles Fluker, one of the leaders of the 21ers.

One of the major challenges in writing this story has been that, by the time I eventually came to take it seriously, a significant amount of time had passed, now more than 50 years. Most of the original participants were dead; of those still living, many could not remember the specifics of the events or the dates. More importantly, as the events unfolded in the early 1960s, most did not see the importance of keeping notes or copies of documents. Especially in the beginning, secrecy, not record keeping, was of paramount importance. Secrecy was of such importance that the organizing was not even discussed at home, except in a couple of cases. In any case, though great, very skilled, intelligent workers, they were not writers and certainly not historians. Even if they kept notes or documents, they were, for the most part, long since forgotten, lost or misplaced when I finally came to this task. The one who probably would have kept the best records, Willie Long, had long been deceased by the time I became more serious about the effort. As far as I have been able to find, his surviving family members have none of his notes or other records. At the time of the episode, most of the participants were probably like me: they did not have the ability to effectively write about the events, even if they had wanted to and/or had recognized the historical importance of the effort, which, apparently, they did not.

I left federal employment at Mare Island in late 1964, vowing never to return. As it turned out, it would be more than 40 years before I set foot on The Shipyard again, but, for reasons that will become obvious, I am glad that I returned. Over the years after 1964, I stayed in touch with some of the 21ers, mainly through James Davis, who had been one of my first instructors when I worked in the nuclear division of Shop 56, what the pipefitters called the "pipe shop." Over the next 35+ years, we sometimes saw each other at sporting events or in nightclubs, and he always invited me to events that the group held, but I did not really participate, feeling that part of my life was behind me. It was a mistake, because, even though I could not have known it at the time, much of what I accomplished later in life was, at some level, related to what I learned through the experience at Mare Island. I should have stayed closer to these great men, but when I left I thought that was the end of any relationship with Mare Island, although, at the personal level, I had no bitter memories. The fact of the matter is that, although I did not know it at the time, the episode and the impression it made would prepare me for a lifelong career largely devoted to or related to African Americans integrating the building trades unions and the construction industry, as a whole, in the San Francisco-Oakland Bay Area. It laid the groundwork for my future work in the areas of affirmative action and social justice in the construction industry. I learned and never forgot the need and necessity for direct action against all forms of discrimination and obstruction to basic rights. .

One of the reasons I left employment at Mare Island was to enroll in full-time college study. Much later, in 1980, after receiving an MA degree in history from San Francisco State University, I began to feel that there was some real historical significance in what the Original 21-25 had done. With that in mind, that year, I traveled from the San Francisco/Oakland Bay Area to Madera, in the Central Valley of California, where I interviewed Willie Long, who had been the leader and driving force in the 21er movement. Part of that interview is still intact. However, because of many personal challenges and changes in circumstance, all of my own making, I let the project drop for many years, although the idea was always "in the back of my mind." Unfortunately, over the course of that time, part of the taped interview was lost, but what remains is important to understanding this story

I became more serious about the project again many years later, in 2002, when James Davis called to invite me to a reunion of sorts of some of the surviving members of the original group. By then, there were not many of us still alive. Of the original group of 25, only eight of us were left, but that was to be expected, because the episode started over 40 years before the reunion. The reunion, held at a Denny's Restaurant in Richmond, was mostly made up of men who were leaders in the organizing and filing of the complaint. Now, in 2016, there are only four of us left.

Until 2006, the story of the 21ers was really only known to and remembered by the surviving participants, and to some extent, those interested in the Naval Archives in San Bruno, California, the archives of the President's Committee on Equal Employment Opportunity (PCEEO) and, possibly, the Hobart Taylor, Jr. papers at the University of Michigan. (Taylor, an African American, was special counsel to the PCEEO). Few, if any, people were interested until that time. As far as I can gather, nowhere in any of the histories of the 1960s and the Civil Rights Movement will one find mention of the 21ers' activities. Even the histories of Mare Island are silent on the 21ers. For example, Sue Lemmon's *Closure: The Final Twenty Years of Mare Island Naval Shipyard* is a book that spans more than 400 pages on the subject of the 20 years preceding the closure of The Shipyard in 1996. There is no mention of the original 21ers or any of its individual members. There is mention of the fact that, in 1986, "with the blessing of the Shipyard Commander and the Deputy Equal Employment Opportunity Officer, efforts began on a project to record the history and progress of African Americans on Mare Island."[2] Ironically, one of the people who volunteered to work on the project was Jesse Bethel, a "prominent" African American who, although employed at Mare Island in 1961, had refused to join with the 21ers. There was absolutely no mention of the original 21ers or any of its individual members. Not one word. There is also discussion of Black History Week and Black History Month. How could there be a Black History Week or Black History Month on Mare Island without a mention of the 21ers, who would have tremendous impact on the opportunities for all African Americans working at Mare Island from 1962 until the time it closed in 1996? This work is meant to be part of the on-going effort to rectify that glaring omission and, to the extent possible, set forth an accurate account of the missing history, to rectify a wrong. It is my strong belief that there is no more important event in the history of African Americans working at Mare Island than the filing of the complaint in 1961, along with subsequent, related events.

A passing conversation began to change things, in terms of recognition. In 2005, in a conversation with his nephew, Anthony Gilmore, Clarence Williams, one of the Original 21ers, casually mentioned the story. Gilmore immediately saw the potential importance of the subject and contacted Matthias Gafni, who was, at the time, a reporter for the *Vallejo Times Herald*. After Gafni followed up with interviews and several articles, the story became generally known in the area and recognition began to pour in for the survivors, culminating in recognition in the Congressional Record and the installation of a memorial stone at Mare Island. However, with no disrespect for Mr. Gafni, I do not think the full story has ever been told or even attempted. This is my attempt, although I do not believe that the complete story will ever be told at this remove from the events. I approach this study with the belief that, across the country, men like pipefitter Willie Long and Charles E. Wilson, the attorney for the 21ers, along with many others, while working out of the limelight, were, in their own ways, as important to the great 20th century civil rights movements as the Martin Luther Kings and Thurgood Marshalls, especially at local levels in the 1950s and 1960s. Their stories, too often, have been left largely untold. This is my effort to tell at least a small part of one story.

By the time that I started again to seriously think about writing the story, in 2003, memories had already faded greatly and, over the almost a decade and a half since then, they have faded even more. In any case, to varying degrees, my telling of the story of the 21ers would have been drastically different if I had written it in 1980, 1990, or 2000. In each period, I was different, the other survivors were different, and the memories were different. The ability to follow up with questions became different and more difficult, as more participants died and memories continued to fade. Along with some limited documentation, this is the story as I and some of the others who were present in the beginning, and through the evolution of events, can now remember it. To my advantage is the fact that, over time, I have gained greater wisdom, knowledge, and experience to bring to bear on the subject.

Although I deeply, deeply regret that it took so long to write this story, I am proud that I was able to complete it at all. To make it possible, I have had great cooperation and support from many others all along the way, some directly and some indirectly.

Aside from this preface, throughout the writing/telling of the story, I have written of myself in the third person. I have done so because I wanted to think and write of myself not as a writer but as an integral part of the group, even though I played a very minor role until we, as a group, started thinking of the value of writing the story. I look upon this writing as a major part of my contribution to the group and to the families of the members.

Why the story? I am told that, according to an old African proverb, when an elder dies, a library is burned. When I die, I want, at least, a part of my library to stand, because I want the story of the Original 21-25 to live and be told forever. It is an important story.

Notes:
1. Twenty-one men signed the complaint one evening in November, 1961. Over the next several days, another four were recruited and agreed to sign.
2. Sue Lemmon, *Closure: The Final Twenty Years of MARE ISLAND NAVAL SHIPYARD.* (Vallejo: Sue Lemmon and Silverback Books, 2001), p. 125.

WILLIE LONG, SR.

OCTOBER 19, 1918 - MAY 13, 1992

CHAPTER 1

Mare Island Naval Shipyard: The Culture and Working Conditions for African Americans, 1930—1961

Before beginning the story, let's fast forward almost 50 years from 1961 for a moment. On November 17, 2010, Jake Sloan was the master of ceremonies for a long anticipated and well attended event to unveil a memorial stone monument to recognize the exploits of a once secretive organization that became known as The Original 21ers and its leader, Willie Long. The ceremony took place in Alden Park, both a somewhat wooded and an open-space setting, on what was formerly Mare Island Naval Shipyard. For more than 100 years, the park has been located on 8th Street, between Railroad and Walnut Avenues, across from and to the west of what is now known as the Historic Core and Shop 56 (in historic Building 46), where from July, 1960 through most of 1964, Jake sometimes worked with Willie Long, John Edmondson and several of the other pipefitters who form part of this story. The little, beautiful and peaceful park is home to memorials to the Marine Corps, to the Navy and to Admiral David Glasgow Farragut, the first commandant of Mare Island and, later, a flag officer in the Civil War, among others. Such recognition was a long time in coming for The Original 21ers. Alden Park is an historic setting for memorializing an historic event. Who was Willie Long and who were the Original 21ers?

Nineteen sixty-one was the year that a future president of the United States, Barack Hussein Obama, a man of partial African descent, was born. That same year, in an obscure city in the San Francisco Bay Area, in what was, for most people, an obscure shipyard, an obscure man by the name of Willie Long was instigating a movement that would help to push forward, if only indirectly, but certainly as part of the cumulative effect, the process by which there would be a Civil Rights Act of 1964 and a progression from there, along with other historical events, to the possibility of Barack Hussein Obama becoming the first African American president of the United States of America. As Mr. Obama clearly states in his book, *The Audacity of Hope; Thoughts on Reclaiming the American Dream*, in reference to the 1960s,"…as the child of a mixed marriage, my life would have been impossible, my opportunities entirely foreclosed, without the social upheavals that were then taking place." [1] It was only a small part of the Civil Rights Movement, but the story of The Original 21ers was, and is, important, especially for African Americans and other minorities who were then working or would later work for the federal government. It is important for history. Who was Willie Long and who were the Original 21ers?

In November of 1961, 25 courageous men, led by Willie Long, who was inspired by the national, regional, and local civil rights movements, as well as his co-worker and mentor, John Edmondson, took an historic step towards ending long-standing and blatant racial discrimination in hiring, placement, training, promotions and equal pay at Mare Island, by filing a complaint against such discrimination at The Shipyard. The complaint was filed with the President's Committee on Equal Employment Opportunity (PCEEO), which was established by President John F. Kennedy's Executive Order 10925 in March, 1961. Over time, and relatively speaking, the complaint would help lead to sweeping changes, locally and, possibly, nationally. Who was Willie Long and who were the Original 21ers, the people that were being recognized that day in 2010? The answer is part of the story that follows.

***

Mare Island lies at the lower reaches of the Napa River, which divides it from the city of Vallejo, California, not far from where it reaches and flows into Carquinez Straits on San Pablo Bay. In 1852, an Act of Congress authorized the establishment of Mare Island Nava Shipyard, which would become the Navy's first yard on the Pacific Coast. Then, in 1853, the Federal Government purchased the island from its three owners for the sum of $83,000. The Act called for the construction of a foundry, machine shop, boiler shop, engine house, pattern house, carpenters shop and storehouses. In 1854, David Glasgow Farragut was assigned to manage the construction and initiation of The Shipyard. Over the years, The Shipyard grew to the point that, during World War II, it was capable of carrying a workforce of more than 46,000, working around the clock, and becoming a part of a great military staging area for activities in the Pacific and Far East. It closed in 1996.

The first African American workers are believed to have started working at Mare Island in the latter part of the 19th century. According to research done by Sharon McGriff-Payne, a local writer who focuses on the history of African Americans in Solano County, "During the first decade of the twentieth century, at least eight African American men served as clerks at Mare Island." [2] However, during and after World War II, the opportunities to work in certain jobs changed, because of the arrival and influence of many of the whites sometimes known as "Okies" (only some of whom came from Oklahoma and some, but most of whom came from some part of the segregated South), who came out of the fields in the Central Valley and some directly from the South. The influx of white Southerners into the shipyards of northern and southern California brought the harder forms and ideas of discrimination that were part of their Southern heritage, including work and pay customs. This had significant impacts. For example, race-tiered pay structures were common in the South, the region of origin for many of the whites, as well as many of the African Americans working at Mare Island. More than likely, many of the older African American workers at Mare Island had worked under such conditions if, indeed, not in some forms of modern day slavery in the South, especially if they had been industrial workers. Those who had been tenant farmers or sharecroppers

may have fared even worse. Both the African Americans and the whites working at Mare Island may have been accustomed to and expecting race-tiered pay
structures as a norm. In addition, according to economist and former Secretary
of Labor Ray Marshall, "whites considered it improper for Negroes to compete
directly with them for better jobs. It was especially unthinkable that Negroes
should hold supervisory positions over them."[3] They also brought with them
ideas about the exclusion of African Americans from certain trades. To be certain, some white workers brought with them their notions of simple fairness to
African Americans. Increasingly, then, over time, although employees of the
Federal Government, African Americans faced increasingly significant discrimination and, although they sometimes worked under a civil service system, it
meant little, in reality, if the leaders on Mare Island wanted to fire any of them
or restrict opportunities for training, advancement or fair pay. They often did
so with virtual impunity. In the end, the culture and beliefs of the South,
strongly influenced by slavery and its Jim Crow successor, with related beliefs,
prejudices and fears, held by both whites and African Americans, would have
tremendous impacts on events as they unfolded in the 1940s, '50s and '60s at
Mare Island. Compounding the matter, often many of the men who made up
the ranks of the naval officer corps, the top managers at Mare Island, were also
from or descended from the South.

Be that as it may, in 1961, a casual observer could easily have believed that
race relations were good or at least acceptable at Mare Island. The casual observer would have been wrong. Yes, there were hundreds, if not thousands, of
African Americans working there and there were few formal complaints of
discrimination. Yes, hundreds, if not thousands, of African Americans were
employed at Mare Island and they appreciated the steady employment and good
benefits paid by the Federal Government and enjoyed by many of them. But
there was deep-seated and long-standing resentment by some over the general
lack of equal opportunity. For example, there were African American men
working in the production shops, classified as helpers, who should have been
promoted to journeyman or "mechanic" years or even decades before they were
or if, indeed, they ever were. There were African American journeymen, men
like John Edmondson, who should have been promoted to the level of leading
man or higher many years before. (In the case of John Edmondson, some be-

lieved that he should have been Master of Shop 56, the pipefitters shop). Thus, there was long standing resentment on the part of some, and, though largely unspoken, it was simmering, becoming hot, ready to boil over.

Discrimination on Mare Island was reflective of the wider, long-standing problem for African Americans working for the Federal Government at the time. Executive Order 8802, also known as the Fair Employment Act, was signed by President Franklin D. Roosevelt on June 25, 1941, an action seeking to provide equal opportunity and prohibit the prevailing racial discrimination in the national defense industry. It was the first federal action, though not a law, to promote equal opportunity and prohibit employment discrimination in the United States. The Order required all federal agencies and departments involved with defense production to ensure that vocational and training programs were administered without discrimination as to "race, creed, color, or national origin."[4] All defense contracts were to include provisions that barred private contractors from discrimination as well. The executive order was issued in response to pressure from civil rights activists, notably Bayard Rustin, A. Philip Randolph, and A. J. Muste, who had planned a march on Washington, D.C., to protest racial discrimination. The Committee on Fair Employment Practice was established by Executive Order 8802 within the Office of Production Management to investigate alleged violations and "to take appropriate steps to redress grievances."[5] The committee was also supposed to make recommendations to federal agencies and to the president on how Executive Order 8802 could be made most effective. The march was suspended after the Executive Order was issued. The Executive Order notwithstanding, however, over the ensuing years until the 21er filing, it had little effect on hiring, training and promotions at Mare Island. There was still significant discrimination in the areas of job placement, training, promotions and equality of pay at Mare Island even in late 1960, but things were "heating up."

***

As it was, in the early 1960s, the situation at Mare Island was reflective of the reality of the lack of employment and promotional opportunities for African Americans throughout the Federal Government at the time. For example, in a report released in 1961, as reported in *Of Kennedys and Kings*, "Of the 6,900 employees in the upper reaches of the Agriculture Department, just 15 were black. At the Pentagon the figure was only 444 of the 69,955 higher grade staff. At the federal Civil Service, only two blacks had the highest-ranking levels of GS 17 and GS 18."[6]

At Mare Island, although the overall number of African Americans employed, at least in some shops, was not necessarily low, there were many, many obstacles to them advancing through training and promotional opportunities. To make matters worse, there was denial of the obvious on the part of the shipyard leadership. As remembered by James "Jim" Davis, then [1962] a journeyman pipefitter in shop 56:

> You know something [is] wrong...but, anyway, the shipyard [man-agement] answer was...the reason that blacks don't get temporary promotions was because they didn't go to social events. Remember that clearly, you know. Pipefitters would have picnics in Napa and shit, you know. Even the guy from Washington talking about it, [said] that was the most ridiculous answer that they could give. [7]

The reality was that, both in 1961 and later, African Americans were not an integral part of the Mare Island culture, either on the island or as it extended to off the shipyard activities. The *Mare Island Grapevine*, known as simply "The Grapevine" among The Shipyard workers, was the official newsletter for the shipyard from 1942 to 1996. It carried many photos of Mare Island related business/work and social activities. Issues of The Grapevine for the period 1959 to 1964 show very few photos of African Americans at all and only one in a position of influence or power. In a book published as late as 1977, *Sidewheels to Nuclear Power*, there are 240 pages of photos, and some text, of buildings, ships and people covering many decades of the history of Mare Island. There are many, many photos of people, alone or in groups. As far as can be determined visually, there is not one photo containing the image of an African American. Not one.

***

At the time of the organizing for and the filing of the complaint, there was a usual and largely accepted progression leading to a leadership position for those working in the production trades/shops. A new employee normally started working at Mare Island as either an apprentice or a helper, if working in the production shops. If one started as an apprentice and successfully completed the training, one automatically became a journeyperson, usually after 4 years. If one started as a helper, usually, the first possible promotion was to the level of "limited" mechanic/journeyperson. The next step was a promotion to mechanic or journeyperson. After either of those two paths, either as a former apprentice or helper, one could become a "snapper," informally supervising a few people. The next step was to the leadingman level, supervising snappers and mechanics. The next step was to quarterman, a position responsible for supervising several leadingmen and reporting to the shop foreman. The next possible promotion was to shop foreman. The shop foreman reported to the Shop Master, which was the top position in each trade. (For a detail of how the shipyard was organized, see Appendix 1.) Most of the African Americans were helpers in all the shops, some after as long as 15 years or more on the job. However, the reality was that the helpers and limited mechanics, most importantly, often did the same work as journeypersons but without comparable pay. "Well, since we opened that bag of worms, ... Jake you can remember this, on [the ship] building way [activity]...the [ship] building way was ran by black riggers," says Jim Davis. "And they were all helpers." Davis goes on to say, "The white guys...the white guys was the mechanics and they was all taking orders [from African American helpers]. We had two or three or at least a couple guys that signed the complaint that were part of that mechanic/ helper type thing."[8] In the same interview, Jake Sloan says that "Well, I know the helpers did a lot of the work in the pipe shop, limiteds, too. Of course, I became limited and we were doing the same work as the pipefitters or the mechanics. There were some black guys that had been there [working as helpers] for years and years."[9] According to Willie Capers, who worked at Mare Island for more than a decade, "I went there as a helper and I left as a helper,"[10] although he often managed certain rigging operations for Shop 72 and was a key player and supervisor in some of the ship building way activities. Unless some kind of change were to take place, many of the African American men who started as apprentices would probably never have risen above the mechanic/journeyman level; some of those who started as helpers never would have risen above the mechanic limited level. Some may have remained helpers for the duration of their careers at Mare Island. Many did. Eventually, some of the African American workers began to think that enough was enough with such practices.

Other African Americans at Mare Island had the same experiences with promotions at higher levels, such as from journeyman/mechanic to supervisor. Boston Banks stated that when he had a score of 96 on an exam, identical to the score of a white person, the white person went to the top of the promotion list and he went to the bottom. "I went into the office that day…and I went by and looked at the list. My supervisor came out and saw me looking at the list and he says, you can't beat city hall, can you? And I told him, MacArthur, I says, you cannot beat them but you can let them know that you don't appreciate what they are doing."[11]

Many of the whites in leadership roles, starting at the top with the shipyard commanders, along with the rank and file, may have thought it only natural that African Americans were paid less than whites for the same or similar work. In many cases, either directly or through their parents or in-laws, they often had their roots in the South, where such practices had always been the general and standard practice. Although many of the African Americans working on Mare Island may have accepted such practices when they were living and working in the South, some were increasingly reluctant to do so in California.

***

In terms of general, overall numbers, some shops had more African American workers than others. Some shops/trades were more exclusionary, just as they were on the outside in the private sectors in the construction building trades. When asked about the small number of African Americans in some shops, Eddie Brady, who became a 21er, said that:

> Well, I think [some in] the machine shop just thought they was too
> good for blacks. It's the only thing that I can think of; they just didn't
> want'em and they didn't make an effort to hire'em. You see, before our
> organization came, there never was a black [in a position] to go out to
> an employment office to hire employees for Shop 31. I think I went
> out one year just after we got the thing going...the next year Foster
> came out and, ah, we was getting some blacks in then, but until then,
> they was passing them over...I remember one supervisor, he wanted
> to penalize this black guy because he stole a car when he was in high
> school. He made a big joke out of it. And I said hey, we'll take him in
> 38 [Outside Machine Shop]...I said you probably stole one too (laugh-
> ter) in high school, you know...I said the man's been in the service...he
> did his duty. We'll take him. He said well, I hope he steal your car...I
> say hey, we gonna put him inside...I think they hired him in 31 [Inside
> Machine Shop] or 38, yeah."[12]

According to Boston Banks, who was, at the time of the filing, a journeyman machinist in Shop 31, "That was it! They did not want blacks in [some]
shop [s]. We weren't supposed to be able to read or write or do any of this han-
dling of machines and making parts and making them to a specific size."[13]

In the same group interview, Clarence Williams went on to say that "there
were jobs they considered white people jobs."[14] Jim Davis remembers that until
the mid-50s, there was only one African American in Shop 11 [Structural] between Mare Island and Hunter's Point Naval Shipyard in San Francisco, a man
named Frank Jackson. The whites simply did not want African Americans in
certain shops. "The reason they didn't want blacks in these shops [was] because
we was black. That's it, I mean that's it. They didn't want to know if you were a
professor or genius or what. When they saw you, they didn't want you in
there."[15]

This rejection of African Americans by certain trades was, again, a reflection and extension of Southern patterns. For example, the Order of United Machinists and Mechanical Engineers, forerunner of the International Association
of Machinists, was organized in Atlanta in 1888. "Colored" people would not be
allowed to become full members until 1948, and then only on a limited basis.

One of the skilled trade shops on Mare Island was somewhat different, at
least to an extent. Shop 56, the pipefitters, had many more African Americans
overall and more African American mechanics than any of the other shops. In

fact, some people thought the African American pipefitters should not be complaining at all. However, the reality was that many of the African Americans in the shop had been helpers for years but could not receive promotions to mechanic or even, in many cases, limited mechanic. And, with one historical exception, none had ever been promoted to supervisor. As it turned, out more African Americans from Shop 56 eventually signed the complaint than from any other shop. This may have resulted from the fact of the strong influence of Willie Long and John Edmondson in the shop, or it may have been a reflection of higher expectations.

There was one other, major, barrier in place to prevent some African Americans from working in or advancing in certain shops, regardless of the numbers of African Americans or the shop. At the time of the filing, many African American temporary employees were unable to become permanent workers, which was a requirement for promotions, Banks said. The long-standing practice was that a day before reaching permanent status, which was one year of continuous employment, the workers would be laid-off on Friday and then rehired on temporary status the next Monday. According to Banks,

> That's right. In the same way with your advancement, you had to have a certain amount of time in this position before they would make you permanent. You never made permanent. You never had that time in the position, to make permanent, so we were more or less left out of everything, because they could cut you off just before you were able to move on. No, you didn't miss any work. They'd bring you out on Friday evening and hire you back Monday morning, if you were just a temporary employee. And you only got a chance to make permanent, if you had a year in. That was standard [practice]. [16]

That practice was known as "broken time," or "broken service." "You would just work a year at a time. One year then [laid]off, [another] year then [laid] off," Banks continued.[17] One had to have more than one year to make permanent status and one had to be permanent to make mechanic, unless one had gone through an apprenticeship. The only exception was for veterans, which helped people such as Boston Banks, Eddie Brady, Willie Capers, Louis Greer and Jake Sloan, all of whom had served honorably in the military.

Although, in most cases, it was out of the question for an African American to be promoted to leading man, for all the reasons stated above, it was difficult to even get a promotion to the position of "snapper." Being a snapper was important, because, even when the African Americans passed a qualifying exam, they were not accepted over the whites who had been snappers. Furthermore, to add insult to injury, in the area of promotions, African Americans were often passed over in favor of whites they had trained. "One week we were training an individual and the next week he was telling you what to do. So we began to become disgruntled," said Willie Long.[18] Some of the workers were familiar with similar stories of working conditions on the outside, in the private sector. Says Jim Davis about his father's experiences, "My dad, he got an attitude where he wouldn't tell whites anything. He said, here comes a guy who doesn't know anything...three weeks, a month, two months, he's the boss. He's bossing you [after] you taught him everything. He said it happened time and time again."[19] According to Long, this was not just true "for blacks but to Orientals, the Mexican Americans. They had nothing; it was only the whites [who] were permitted to hold certain jobs."[20]

On issues of discrimination, more important than anything, however, were the general facts "on the ground," the generalized discrimination that was faced by the African Americans on Mare Island on a daily basis. According to Jim Davis: "There is no way we could tell you the horror stories we experienced over there [at Mare Island]. At every phase of each work day, we ran into discrimination."[21] And the indignities and racism to be faced on Mare Island took many forms, some large, some small. For example, the whites were always asking African Americans if they were "getting enough," meaning enough sex. Jake Sloan's standard response was "are you missing any?" On at least one occasion, a white man asked Sloan whether he preferred sex with white women or African Americans. Sloan's answer was that he did not know, because he had never had sex with an African American woman. Such answers usually ended the ridiculous discussions, at least for a while.

***

The story of John Edmondson is, at some level, probably most typical of the problems that had been evolving for years at Mare Island, especially at the level of promotions. He was widely respected and had great influence with the African American workers on Mare Island and so his story is important in understanding the big picture background to what unfolded.

Edmondson was born in Memphis, Tennessee, in 1908. His family sent him to California "to keep him alive" when he finished high school, recalls his daughter, Catherine Edmondson-Fulcher.[22] Apparently, John always took pride in himself and spoke up for his rights, which could put him in great danger in the South. He was a tough guy who, according to Jim Davis, was a star on a very good Mare Island football team in the 1930s. Edmondson had relatives in Vallejo and the area, one of whom was an uncle, George Posey, a Buffalo Soldier who had come to Vallejo in the early 1900s, according to Sharon McGriff-Payne.

Edmondson began his apprenticeship at Mare Island in 1930 and later became one of the best if not the best among the journeyman pipefitters in Shop 56. At one point, it was said that he and Daryl Franklin, another African American pipefitter, could dismantle and then repair the piping system on a ship without any help. That is probably a stretch but they were outstanding pipefitters. However, his skill notwithstanding, Edmondson's career was full of challenges and discrimination, as would be the case for Franklin, although, for a unique reason, he was ultimately more fortunate in receiving a promotion. Over the years, Edmondson repeatedly voiced his dissatisfaction with the lack of promotional opportunities for African Americans, but could never get the support he needed from other African Americans in order to take real action. According to Jim Davis and others, many years before 1961, Edmondson had tried to organize African Americans to protest the discrimination at Mare Island. Because of their ultimate lack of courage to stand up, he repeatedly met with failure. Because of this lack of courage among the African Americans and the ongoing discrimination, Edmondson had become somewhat embittered long before the 1960s.

By 1960, then, Edmondson had been working on Mare Island for 30 years. Regarded by most as a first rate pipefitter, if not the best on The Shipyard, he had never been promoted to Leading Man [supervisor], although some of the white supervisors in his shop were barely born when he came to The Shipyard. In some cases, they had been trained on-the-job under his direction. To a lesser extent, the same was true for many other African Americans working at Mare Island at the time. However, more than most others, Edmondson was widely admired and respected, especially by African Americans, but even by whites. Of him, Boston Banks said:

> Yeah, he was in Shop 56. I had met him and talked with him. I knew he was a good mechanic and all the whites spoke highly of him. I really admired him. He would work. He would do a beautiful job. Everybody would go to him if they had a problem, [and] that included white mechanics. They would go to him because John was a pipefitter and he was a good one.[23]

Since he was considered to be an outstanding pipefitter, at one point he was promoted to the position of "snapper." However, he could never get a promotion to the position of leadingman, nor could other African Americans, with very few exceptions, in almost none of the numerous production shops on The Shipyard. In this connection, according to Jim Davis,

> Well, as I recall, we had a ceiling on Mare Island. Not only was it called a glass ceiling, at that time it was a ceiling where there were no blacks that was promoted in any shops. There was only, at that time, approximately two black supervisors, [and] that was in the paint shop and, I guess, sandblasters and riggers. Was that right? No, it wasn't the riggers, it was the sandblasters.[24]

Both on and off Mare Island, signs of discrimination, direct or indirect, were everywhere and were long-standing. In 1961, there were people still working at the yard who were old enough to remember the Ku Klux Klan activities in Vallejo. One such man was John Edmondson. Also, when Edmondson was serving his apprenticeship, there were still colored and white restrooms on The Shipyard, according to Willie Long. It all bothered him and, according to Long, Edmondson had told him that "several times in his career he had gone up to [the main office of Shop 56] to protest and he would have a bunch around him who would [claim] to want to do something, so they would say, but when he would go up to face the music, he would look around and there was nothing, no one, nobody to back him up."[25] Promotions or not, in everything Edmondson did, according to Jake Sloan, "he carried himself as a proud man and that pride could not be disturbed."[26] Of Edmonson's work and professionalism, Jim Davis remembered Daryl Franklin saying that "if John had been a white man he would have been master of Shop 56."[27] He would not willingly "take low" to any man, under any circumstances.

***

Whichever trade or shop it was, even if an African American could be promoted to mechanic/journeymen, which was not easy, that was basically the end of the line. According to Banks,

> I had seen what was going on. I mean, you take a shop with a thousand people, eleven hundred and some people in it, and you don't have any blacks in it, two blacks, at the most. And we're mechanics then, there has to be something wrong and I was, more or less, told that mechanic is it. You won't be anything else. That is it. You are going to be a mechanic and nothing else.[28]

Davis believes that, among what were considered the "skill" trades, there were more African Americans in the pipe shop [Shop 56] than the other skill trade shops, but there were no African American supervisors and, in 1961, no black snappers, complained Jim Davis. At first, Davis was not upset at the lack of opportunity for promotions, because he was so excited about completing his apprenticeship and becoming a journeyman in 1956. Like many others, he had been lulled into thinking that he should be satisfied with completing an apprenticeship and having a "good" job as a mechanic. That is understandable. As mentioned above, his father worked on the outside, in the private sector, where he could attest to the fact that opportunities for African Americans in some trades were dismal to non-existent. For an indication of the extent of discrimination in the building trades, in 1950, there were 2,190 non-white apprentices in the United States. In 1960, there were 2,191. In 1960, "there were only 79 non-white apprentices in the plumbers and pipefitters trades."[29] *This was for the whole United States.* But, Davis continued, "the more I talked to guys like Charlie Fluker and Johnny Edmondson, I started to realize that, things were not as I saw them, things wasn't as glorified as I once thought." At a meeting in 2003, he went on to say that, "One of the major problems was that, although we had experience, [when] we made the mechanic grade or whatever experience was for the next step, we could not make it." Furthermore, "There was no one above first line supervision, and then the mechanical [skill] shops such as pipe fitters, machinists, electricians and so forth there was no [African American] supervisors at all." Davis finished, in exasperation by saying that, "There was no limited, no, what you call it, they call it snappers, but what type of mechanic was that? The other was somewhere between the supervisor and the working guy."[30]

According to Clarence Williams, his case was almost strictly personal, although he was also concerned about African American progress in general. He did not like the idea that he had people who were working for him but he wasn't paid as a supervisor. He would sometimes be the lead mechanic over the job, but then those who had worked for him would get promoted over him, "and I didn't like that at all. I felt that, you know, my prestige lived at my house. I was there [at Mare Island] to bring back dollar bills, that meant, that meant the higher up you were on scale, the more money you made, a better living for my family."[31] It also was personal with Matthew "Matt" Barnes. The first African American to do so in his shop, he had gone through an apprenticeship and become a journeyman machinist before serving in the military. At Mare Island, he was interested in getting an assignment that had meaning. However, "I was assigned, mostly as a gopher, you know, go for this and go for that, and I was not getting quality kind of jobs, so that was personal with me, and so I confronted my supervisor about it at that time."[32] When he complained, there was resentment and pushback, and "they dumped a whole bunch of plans in front of me and says, ok, so you're so big, so smart, go do this job" with no clear direction.[33] In 1961, Barnes had been "detailed" to become supervisor, in effect becoming a temporary or probationary supervisor, which would eventually, had it taken place, have made him the first African American supervisor in the history of Shop 38. He was detailed for six months along with a white worker. When his six months of temporary time was over, with no real explanation, he was returned to being a mechanic. After a few days, Barnes noticed that John

Santi, the other man who had been detailed at the same time, had never taken the stripe off his hat, which meant he was still serving as a supervisor and, incidentally, would go on to become head of the shop in later years. "That was the awareness to me that something was wrong with this picture." It was about this time that Willie Long came along and "during that time, hearing, you know, Willie's complaint and all the other complaints that [were] coming, recognizing, hey, you know, this is a real problem. We need put ourselves together to address this."[34] He registered his own internal complaint but also decided to follow Willie Long, who was beginning to increasingly agitate for change at the larger level.

Opportunities for specialized training, which could normally help lead to promotions, were also limited for African Americans. Furthermore, even if they had the training, usually it made no difference for promotional opportunities. During that time, when the building of nuclear submarines was a growing effort at Mare Island, men were being sent to specialized, technical training related to the work. African Americans were not offered such training opportunities, even if they were known to be studious. And they were not given credit for what they had done on their own. For example, Jim Colbert, an African American working in Shop 64 (Electrical), was always going to night school to advance his knowledge. According to Jim Davis, when this was brought to the attention of the leadership in discussions about training opportunities and promotions, the response was "well, his education didn't count because he [Jim] was one that just liked to go to school (laughing). And so, one of my principal statements issued to the shipyard commander when we was meeting was that, education was only relevant to blacks when you didn't have it. If you had it, they said, oh well, oh well."[35] Is there any wonder that Colbert would readily sign the complaint when given the opportunity?

Even in the shops that were not thought of as requiring "skill" training, shops such as painting, for example, there was still tremendous discrimination in promotions. The experience of Louis Greer is a good example. When Greer, an African American, was working in the paint shop in the 1950s and early 1960s, there were no African American supervisors. In fact, the only shops that had African American supervisors were the sandblasters and the laborers, according to what was said by Greer in an interview conducted in 2008. In more ways than one, Greer felt that he and others were being discriminated against and be made his feelings known to his supervisor. Getting no results, he somehow wrangled a meeting with Admiral Honsinger, the Shipyard Commander at the time, which was followed by other meetings. Of the first meeting, Greer recalls:

> Yeah, I went to him and I had asked him about the discrimination we were having at Mare Island. We went around a couple of times. One day, he had me in and he said, Greer, I'm going to go down on the low end of the yard with a fine tooth comb. If I don't find no discrimination, I'm going to fire you. So I looked at him and said, Admiral, you don't have to go way down to the low end of the yard. You can go right down the hallway here. It's lily white. And he told me he had nothing to do with the hiring. His claim was there was no discrimination. So, in other words, I said, [for you] to fire me, I got to do something and I'm not going to do anything, so I don't think you can fire me, just because we are having this problem with discrimination. So that was all that was said at that time.[36]

Greer felt that Honsinger only met with him to keep him from writing letters to Washington, which he had already done on a couple of occasions. When the opportunity presented itself, Greer was more than happy to join forces with Willie Long and others, seeking potential strength in numbers.

***

As time went by, both before and after the 21er complaint was filed, there were always attempts to divide and conquer. For example, Jim Davis was told by some reluctant African Americans that the Shop 56 Master, Irwin Whitthorne, liked him and that if he had gone to him and asked, Whitthorne would have given him what he wanted. Davis did not believe it, nor did Sloan. "That was probably one of the reasons, the thing that really frustrated some people was because Whitthorne *did* like you, but it didn't make any difference," Sloan told Davis in the 2003 interview. "He liked you, but you were still black and if I remember correctly, he said there would never again be a black leading man in that shop."[37] Sloan remembered that it was one of the first important, relevant things that he heard on The Shipyard on the issue of race and equal opportunity. It was important, because Whitthorne was probably the most influential civilian on Mare Island at the time. What he thought and said carried great weight. The statement was one of the things that inspired Sloan and some others to step up. Sloan heard the statement recounted from Edmondson, Davis, and Fluker, all of whom he greatly respected. He did not like how the statement sounded or what it implied for the future.

A look at Whitthorne is a good look at the culture and leadership at Mare Island at the time of the organizing. Whitthorne, who had begun his career as a helper and material runner, had worked his way up through the ranks to become probably the most powerful non-naval officer person on The Shipyard and one of the most powerful men in Vallejo, in general, if not the most powerful. He had help in getting there. His father worked in an influential position on Mare Island, as Chief Clerk of the Labor Board. In fact, the family was so well connected that Whitthorne took his first name from Admiral J. Irwin, a Naval Commander of the Asiatic Squadron in the late nineteenth century. At the time of the complaint, Whitthorne was the highest ranking civilian working for the Navy and known as "Mr. Mare Island." Beginning work at The Yard in 1908, by the early 1960s, he had become the dean of civil service employees throughout the Navy and one of the few people to be awarded the Defense Department's Distinguished Civil Service Medal. He was "The Man." The library/archive in the Mare Island Museum contains many articles on Witthorne's life and accomplishments. According to an editorial in the *Vallejo Times Herald* newspaper, at the time of his death in 1973, "Beyond his professional career which brought him so many honors, Irv Whitthorne was a dedicated citizen, a warm and friendly person who was willing to work on projects which might help his city or his fellow man."[38] Nowhere in the editorial or any articles reviewed by this writer is there any mention of Whitthorne raising his voice on the issue of equal opportunity in training, promotions, or pay at Mare Island. Since he was easily the most powerful civilian on The Shipyard, if he had so desired, he probably could have helped to change things for African Americans working there. He did not, neither before nor after the 21er complaint was filed.

***

General and specific discrimination was the reality in the workplace condi-tions for African Americans working on Mare Island in the period leading up to 1961. However, although discrimination at The Shipyard was deliberate and rampant, working there carried a certain amount of almost great prestige in the surrounding African American communities. Many of the African Americans working at Mare Island had come to the West to escape menial, agricultural and industrial work that sometimes actually verged on or became slavery work in the South. Many, many of the African American workers were angry, but most were also very afraid of losing what was considered to be a "good job" at The Shipyard. They considered themselves fortunate to be working at Mare Island. Since professional opportunities were very, very limited to a very great extent, working at places like the Mare Island and Hunters Point Naval ship-yards was seen to be a good opportunity, not only for "good" jobs but stable income for the workers. A job in the shipyards could prove to be a major step-ping stone for an African American family to move into the lower middle class and, possibly, beyond. As such, some of the workers were, to a great extent, intimidated by the real possibility of losing those jobs. As a practical matter, in the 1950s and 1960s, for most African Americans, working at the shipyard, or in any federal job, for that matter, was considered to be a great opportunity, because of the relative job security, especially for veterans. And, beyond the discrimination, the work conditions and benefits were, relatively speaking, very attractive for laborers and craftsmen when measured against jobs available for African American in the private sector. Working in the trades for the Navy was an opportunity not to be taken lightly, because it was extremely difficult for African Americans to enter into the building trades unions in non-governmental work. People like Jake Sloan could get a job at Mare Island, even in the skill trade shops, if they could pass the basic exam in place at the time, which was not very difficult. However, once on the job, even though there was relative job security for many, there was still rampant discrimination. Be that as it may, at bottom, many of the African American workers saw this protest, led by Willie Long, as a step that could threaten their best means of economic sur-vival. "We understood that reality and we had the same fears but it did not stop us," notes Jake Sloan.[39]

For some, the frustration and anger over all the lack of equal opportunity showed itself in many ways. Pilferage on the part of African Americans working at Mare Island was common, even when what was stolen was often not needed and not of much value. For some of the African American workers, this was often seen as just a way of "getting back" at "the man" for real or perceived injustices in working conditions, promotional opportunities and unequal pay. It was a common feeling in the workplace, both on Mare Island and elsewhere at the time. For example, pilferage by African American longshoremen working at Bay Area ports was commonplace. In another area, in talking about petty stealing while growing up in Oakland, Huey Newton, leader of the Black Panther Party, writing of when he was a young man, noted that, "We did not feel that stealing...was wrong. We were getting back at people who made us feel small and insignificant at a time when we needed to feel important and hopeful."[40]

However, by 1961, such weak, symbolic protest was not enough for a small but growing number of the African American workers at Mare Island. The foundations for action that went back many years would come to a head in 1961. Looming on the horizon and prepared for action was the formidable and fearless Willie Long.

Increasingly, then, some of the men wanted more than the "good" jobs that satisfied many if not most of the African American workers, especially in the short run but also in the long-term. Although these men took great pride in having a "good" job with benefits or in becoming a journeyman or "mechanic," in the jargon of the shipyard workers, they also wanted to be paid fairly for the work they did and to be treated fairly in training and promotional opportunities.

At some level, a great part of what drove the men was pride, but, as Eddie Brady said, "So, hey, I wanted all kind of improvement. Anyway, like Mr. Williams said, the dollar was the thing. If you get more pay, you lived better."[41] In order to get more pay without working overtime, one had to be able to get promotions. But it was even more than that. What the 21ers were pushing for was *race free* equal opportunities for employment, training, promotions and pay.

As Willie Long watched, listened, pondered, and seethed, such were the conditions at Mare Island in the years leading up to 1960 and 1961. At least three external realities were to have influence on Long and the 21ers: the local and national social, political, and economic climate, the Civil Rights Movement, and the negative African American relationship with organized labor, especially the construction building trades unions.

Notes:

1. Barack Obama, *The Audacity of Hope: Thoughts on Reclaiming the American Dream*. (New York: Three Rivers Press, 2006), p.29.
2. Sharon McGriff-Payne, *John Grider's Century: African Americans in Solano, Napa and Sonoma Counties from 1845 to 1925*. (New York: iUniverse, Inc., 2009). p. 64.
3. Ray Marshal, *The Negro and Organized Labor*. (New York: John Wiley & Sons, Inc., 1965), p. 64.
4. Executive Order 8802. June 25, 1941.
5. Ibid.
6. Harris Wofford, *Of Kennedys and Kings: Making Sense of the Sixties*. (Pittsburg: University of Pennsylvania Press, 1980), p. 213.
7. Boston Banks, Matthew Barnes, Eddie Brady, Willie Capers, James Davis, Jake Sloan, Clarence Williams, in recorded interview by Jake Sloan. March 22, 2003, Richmond, California.
8. Ibid.
9. Ibid.
10. Ibid.
11. Ibid.
12. Ibid.
13. Ibid.
14. Ibid.
15. Ibid.
16. Ibid.
17. Ibid.
18. Willie Long, in recorded interview by Jake Sloan. July 3, 1980, Madera, California.
19. Boston Banks and James Davis, in recorded interview by Jake Sloan. July 2, 2004, Vallejo, California.
20. Willie Long interview.

21. *Vallejo Times Herald.* November 12, 2006, p. A3.

22. Catherine Edmondson-Fulcher, in recorded interview by Jake Sloan. March 5, 2007, Vallejo, California.

23. Banks, Davis interview.

24. Ibid.

25. Willie Long interview.

26. Jake Sloan, *Notes and Reminiscences.* Unpublished.

27. Banks, Barnes, *et al* interview.

28. Banks, Davis interview.

29. Jake Sloan, *Blacks in Construction.* Unpublished MA Thesis.

30. Banks, Davis interview.

31. Clarence Williams interview.

32. Banks, Barnes, *et al* interview.

33. Matthew Barnes, in recorded interview by Jake Sloan. June 23, 2004, Richmond, California.

34. Banks, Barnes, *et al* interview.

35. Banks, Barnes, *et al* interview.

36. Louis Greer, in recorded interview by Jake Sloan. February 20, 2008, Berkeley, California.

37. Jake Sloan, *Notes and Reminiscences.*

38. *Vallejo Times Herald,* June 22, 1973 editorial page.

39. Jake Sloan, *Notes and Reminiscences.*

40. Huey P. Newton, *Revolutionary Suicide.* (New York: Penguin Books, 1973), p. 26.

41. Banks, Barnes, *et al* interview.

John Edmondson (left) and Daryl Franklin, Mare Island, 1945

CHAPTER 2

Organizing: The Political and Social Environment

More than Willie Long's desires and aspirations would be required for success in facing and confronting the problems at Mare Island. In a general sense, the right consciousness had to be in place to support him. The timing was right, for many reasons. Perhaps not completely right, but enough so. The mid-to-late 1950s and the early 1960s was a period of increasing activity in the area of civil rights, at the local, state and national levels. Most of the attention was on the Southern states but there was also activity at the western regional and local levels, including in the San Francisco/Oakland Bay Area. All influenced the thinking of some of the African Americans working at Mare Island, especially Willie Long and the workers that he would need to support him.

At the national level, at the time, much of the political leadership in the United States Congress was not especially sympathetic to the needs or problems facing African Americans. For an example of the fairly dominant thinking, even many years later, Barry Goldwater, a US senator at the time, could write of Richard Russell "The gentleman from Georgia with the homespun face and courtly manner was a brilliant legal scholar and historian."[1] There was no mention of the fact that the gentleman with the courtly manner was a blatant, "card-carrying" racist of the first magnitude. Goldwater himself voted against the 1964 Civil Rights Bill and, as did future president George H. W. Bush. Later, Goldwater voted against making Martin Luther King's birthday a national holiday. Goldwater was, like many others, a symbol of his times. The reality was that, at the time, most Caucasians in the United States, at all levels, were more than a little comfortable with racism.

However, 1960 brought to the political center stage three men who, for various reasons, were to have a tremendous impact on the lives of African Americans in the coming years and decades: Lyndon Baines Johnson, Richard Milhous Nixon and John Fitzgerald Kennedy respectively, born and reared in the South, the West and the Northeast. All, in one way or another, influenced the move toward increased civil rights and their related effects on African Americans. Both directly and indirectly, Johnson may have been the one to have the most impact/influence on Willie Long and his followers, especially in the short term, through his role as chair of the PCEEO, but also in the long-term through pushing for various bills on civil rights.

With the election of John F. Kennedy, there still was not much leadership at the presidential level on issues of civil rights for African Americans, just as had been the case under presidents Harry Truman and Dwight Eisenhower. Although the African American vote was significant in getting John Kennedy elected, beyond lip service, he was not a strong supporter of civil rights or equal employment opportunity as he ran for office or in his first couple of years as president. According to Juan Williams, in his book *Thurgood Marshall: American Revolutionary*, "...Marshall did not like Bobby Kennedy and considered both Kennedys [Bobby and John] lacking genuine commitment to civil rights at home or in Africa."[2] It has been said that Kennedy believed that, at times, illusion is more important than reality. For the most part, at least in the beginning, that was his approach to civil rights. Although African Americans were prominent in his inaugural events and even though some were appointed to visible positions in his administration, at bottom, he was more concerned with Southern political support than with addressing the root causes of segregation, discrimination and their effects on African Americans. In the early 60s, there were still liberal Republicans in the Senate who supported civil rights, including Jacob Javits and Kenneth Keating, both of New York. But Kennedy was often more concerned with placating southern Democrats, who were often chairs of key committees. For example, J. William Fulbright, a known racist and segregationist from Arkansas, was Kennedy's first choice for Secretary of State, to the dismay of many. To African American reporters, the idea was especially disappointing because "—they had been told during the campaign that the Nobel Prize-winning Black diplomat Ralph Bunch was earmarked for the job."[3] Although Fulbright declined, getting Kennedy off the hook, this was an early indicator of his inclinations, as was his consideration of Ernest Vandeveer of Georgia for Secretary of the Army. Vandeveer was known to be much more of an outspoken segregationist than Fulbright. Even the ideas for executive orders affecting civil rights to circumvent a southern dominated, racist and recalcitrant congress came mainly from Harris Wofford, a top advisor to Kennedy. Such observers as former baseball player Jackie Robinson felt that Kennedy was weak on knowledge of and commitment to civil rights. For the most part, in 1960, and the first years of his presidency, any commitment that Kennedy had for civil rights apparently was driven strictly by his desire to become and remain president. The truth is that, in his first years in congress, Kennedy had been supportive of civil rights but, over time, the southerners beat him down. In addition, he needed them more as president than he did as either a congressman or a senator. But it probably went beyond politics, in some cases. In the 1950s and 1960s, Kennedy's best friend was George Smathers, the anti-civil rights senator from Florida. Kennedy was also good friends with Richard Russel, arch conservative and racist. At bottom, it appears that Kennedy was a practical, calculating politician, and that racism and civil rights were not his priorities in any sense, at least not in the early 1960s.

***

In the minds of the general public, in the area of civil rights, most of the attention was focused on the Southern states, but there was activity at the local, regional and state levels in California. In the 1950s and 1960s, however, such cities as Oakland, Richmond and Vallejo, where many of the African American workers lived, unlike an Atlanta, Georgia, for example, did not have the needed strong infrastructure, the thriving African American institutions, the banks, insurance companies, other businesses, newspapers, churches, and educational institutions, whose leaders were part of a powerful African American economic and social elite. Basically, other than the churches, there were few such African American institutions for the workers to draw upon for support at the immedi-

ately local level, the East Bay or North Bay communities. Nor was there a significant professional class to draw upon, for the most part. This was certainly
true of Richmond and Vallejo and, to a lesser extent, Oakland. As far as can be
determined from this vantage point, there were no significant African American business associations of note at the time. The closest to it was probably Men
of Tomorrow, an Oakland based social and political organization with members
from around the Bay Area. Even a few of the African Americans who worked at
Mare Island, including Charlie Fluker, who would become a 21er, belonged to
Men of Tomorrow, but it was not a significant force for economic or social
change, although some of the members, men such as Al McKee and C. J. Patter-
son, pushed for addressing economic development issues for African Americans. There were few, if any, college professors or lawyers to give theoretical or
strategic assistance, even if willing. African American attorney Charles Wilson,
who was to work with the 21ers, was an exception, although not the only one.

In general, the National Association for the Advancement of Colored People
(NAACP) was very active on these issues at the time, but in many of the chapters of the Bay Area, especially in the late 50s and early 60s, there was a lot of
infighting between moderates and progressives in the various chapters, particularly the chapter in San Francisco, which was controlled by attorney Terry
Francois, a future member of the San Francisco Board of Supervisors, and Willie Brown, future speaker of the Assembly and Mayor of San Francisco.

And so, at bottom, the *Brown vs. Board of Education*, decision, the Civil
Rights Acts of 1957 and 1958 and heightened civil rights activities notwith-
standing, by 1960, little had been done to advance the cause of full freedom and
economic improvement for African Americans anywhere in the United States.
Jobs of any kind were difficult to find, especially for those with little education.
According to Jake Sloan,

> Most of us were just trudging along, doing the best we could under the
> circumstances. Most of us just wanted a job, any kind of job. I took the
> first one that came along, starting to work at Mare Island Naval Ship-
> yard a short while after I was discharged from the Army in July, 1960.[4]

Also, in looking at the challenges facing a group like the 21ers, the reality
was that many of those in the "leadership" of the Civil Rights Movement were

living in a different world from those struggling on the ground. For example, when the 21ers were organizing in 1961, Whitney Young of the Urban League was at Harvard on a $1,000 per month fellowship. Thurgood Marshall with the NAACP Legal Defense Fund had been making $10,000 per year as far back as the late 1940s. Starting pay for helpers at Mare Island at the time of the organizing was $1.98 an hour, which was thought to be decent money for the African American working class at the time, especially for one just starting a working career with little formal education, as was the case with Sloan and many others.

Nevertheless, with all the challenges still in place, by the beginning of the 1960s, the Civil Rights Movement was gaining great momentum. According to *Miami Herald* columnist Leonard Pitts, "As far as social justice is concerned, of course, the 1960s stand second only to the 1860s as the most profoundly transformative decade of American history,"[5] especially for blacks. It was an interesting time for young African Americans in the Bay Area. Many were of the first generation to come of age in the "Promised Land." It was a time of great and increasing agitation over discrimination in employment and housing. Civil rights activities in the area resulted in the passage of the 1959 Fair Employment Practices Act to address employment discrimination against African Americans in California. The struggle for fair housing began in the late 50s and early 60s and culminated in the passage of the Rumford Fair Housing Act in 1963.

***

In 1960 and 1961, some of the African Americans working at Mare Island were reading about all that was happening across the country in the area of civil rights, and, in particular, at the western regional level, they were reading about demonstrations in Los Angeles, mainly sponsored by the NAACP. Also, some of them were reading about the events taking place in San Francisco, such as the pickets against the hotels, restaurants, and car dealerships that were failing to hire African Americans. That is, through it all, they were seeing the real and potential benefits of direct action with public support, at the national, regional and local levels.

The ongoing and ever-present discrimination notwithstanding, there was still a feeling of great excitement and hope in the air in California. Governor

Pat Brown was dreaming and talking of directing a move to more affordable higher education, fair housing and the final construction of the California Aqueduct. In time, all of this would benefit African Americans, helping with the creation of an extended middle class with more African American participation. The organizers at Mare Island saw and felt all of this as evidence of the potential for change.

Great excitement notwithstanding, in the Bay Area, it was a time of great challenges in the areas of discrimination and segregation, especially in the areas of housing and employment. At the time, most, if not all, of the cities in the Bay Area were like Oakland, where the Knowland family ruled and where, as described in *Killing the Messenger: The Story of Radical Faith, Racism's Backlash, and the Assassination of a Journalist,* "They treated Negroes as a nuisance."[6] Police brutality was common, often driven by white racist officers recruited from Southern states. At bottom, in the area of racial relations, fair housing and employment opportunities, Vallejo, like other cities, remained a great challenge in the early 60s. The *Vallejo Times-Herald,* the local newspaper, employed no African Americans. None of the banks employed African Americans. None of the department stores employed African Americans. The police departments and their officers were adamantly racist, even if there were a few African Americans serving on the forces. If a few African Americans were hired, it was with a clear understanding that they were to help control the Africa American community. Much the same was true for Berkeley, Oakland and Richmond, all home to many of the African Americans who worked at Mare Island.

But, still, there was movement. San Francisco was a great example of the struggles. Willie Brown was one of the African Americans leading the struggle to integrate housing and end discrimination in hiring in the city. Berkeley was the home base of Byron Rumford, who was to lead the fight for fair employment and housing policies at the state level.

However, for the organizers at Mare Island, in all likelihood, aside from direct support, much of the outside, off The Island, local inspiration for Long and the others, probably came directly from what was happening in Richmond and Oakland. About half of those who became 21ers lived in, and probably found inspiration from, what was happening in those two cities at the time.

Several of the men who became 21ers and lived outside Vallejo car-pooled together, driving mainly from Richmond and Oakland, with a few from Berkeley. This made active and on-going communication much easier at a time when there was no such thing as a conference call, FAX or email.

A relatively large number of the African Americans working in the production shops on Mare Island lived in Richmond, and they were to have a high level of influence within the 21er group. Since the 1940s, Richmond had been the home of an extremely activist branch of the NAACP. For the carpoolers, all of whom belonged to the NAACP, the drive from Richmond to and then parking on Mare Island took about 30 minutes, plenty of time for conversations often filled with exchanges about current events and, in particular, about the Civil Rights Movement and the related working conditions at Mare Island. Some of the men who lived in Richmond also patronized Greer's Barber Shop, located at 4th and Grove Streets in North Richmond, in the heart of the African American community. At Greer's, along with sports, the conversation between the barbers and their customers often turned to the Civil Rights Movement, at both the national and local levels. Here, in addition to the time spent together carpooling, some of the men talked and compared notes. Also adding to their knowledge pool, many from Richmond had dealt with the discrimination in the shipyards during and after World War II. According to Sacramento State University history professor Shirley Ann Wilson Moore, "...the [Richmond] shipyard experience helped black Richmondites develop political and social proficiencies that gave them a new perspective on their place in Richmond, the state and the nation."[7] She goes on to state that the activism that had taken place in Richmond during the 1940s and early 1950s had "generated and reinforced a cult of expectations among the African Americans in Richmond."[8] Probably partly driven by this combination, about a third of the men who became 21ers were from Richmond. Matthew Barnes, Willie Capers, Charles Fluker, Jimmie James, Matthew Luke, Jake Sloan, Brodie Taylor, and Clarence Williams, all lived in Richmond and all had carpooled together at one time or another. Four of them-Fluker, James, Luke and Sloan-worked in the Pipe Shop, where John Edmondson and Willie Long also worked.

The African American community in Oakland, where Willie Long had lived for a number of years, had been very active on issues of civil rights since at least the period right after World War II. There, Long was a member of the choir at Taylor Memorial Methodist Church, which was actively involved in many programs focused on the uplifting of the African American community. As a prime example of activism in Oakland, the Brotherhood of Sleeping Car Porters, which dated back to the 1920s, had a fairly large contingent of its members living in Oakland. In their activism, the porters had a rather significant influence across the country, sometimes direct and sometimes indirect. In Montgomery, Alabama, it was direct in the person of E.D. Nixon. In Oakland, it was direct in the person of C. L. Dellums and his followers. Dellums had been part of the team that started negotiations with the Pullman Company years before, in 1935, dealing with issues somewhat similar to those facing the African American workers at Mare Island. In addition to the activism of the porters, as reported by Robert O. Self in *American Babylon: Race and the Struggle for Postwar Oakland*:

> Oakland was…a major seat of African American influence in California politics beginning in the late 1940s and the home of an extensive tradition of black social advocacy and organizing. Indeed, the generation of black activists, long before the rise of the [Black] Panthers, developed strategies, alliances, and sources of power that profoundly shaped the political terrain of race in both the East Bay and California as a whole."[9]

Charles Fluker, who would become one of the 21ers, was a member of Men of Tomorrow, the social action and limited economic empowerment group that was centered in Oakland, as was attorney Wilson, who was also an influential member of the East Bay Democratic Club, an African American political organization.

Essentially, because of the combination of knowledge of what was going on in the Civil Rights Movement at all levels, along with local activism, there was a raised level of consciousness among some of the Mare Island African American workers, which Long could draw upon in organizing and then bring to bear in challenging the powers that prevailed on The Island. There was a belief that, even if there were only a small group to start with, it would grow over time, based on that increased and growing level of consciousness. This proved to be only partially true.

***

One thing was certain and the African American workers on Mare Island were fully aware of it: They could not depend on organized labor for support, and that was particularly true of the building and construction trades unions. They saw no opportunity for alternative jobs or support from the building trades. Some people may have thought that African Americans should have been able to count on organized labor for support, but those with any real understanding of the extent of racism in the labor movement had learned otherwise. People such as A. Phillip Randolph, of the Brotherhood of Sleeping Car Porters, understood that, although labor was a central pillar of the American power structure, one supposedly constructed around the lofty principles of equality and democracy, the reality was that he also knew that organized labor's racist treatment of black workers made a mockery of its founding precepts. Locally, African Americans had a long negative history with labor, going back over many decades and, as such, would not have depended on them to help lead the cause, especially those who had worked in and faced rampant discrimination in the shipyards of Richmond and other cities in the Bay Area during and immediately after the Second World War. In addition, historically, the building trades unions may have been the most recalcitrant in giving opportunities to African Americans. It may be worthy of note that the African American organizers at Mare Island never considered forming a union. For most trades, the ability of African Americans to join a union was pretty much out of the question.

There was always antagonism between organized labor, African American workers and activists. One of the reasons, beyond sheer racism, was the fact that organized labor thought that African Americans were strike breakers, which, of necessity, they were at times. As such, even as late as 1960, some of the unions still had racial barriers written into their constitutions. It was so bad that, as Marshall notes, "In 1950 A. Phillip Randolph and other Negro-American union leaders formed the Negro-American Labor Council (NALC) which sought, among other things, to fight discrimination from within the labor movement."[10] This was all at the national level.

But the workers also had local, first-hand knowledge of challenges to integrating the building trades. The knowledge base went beyond what was found in the shipyards. The late Ray Dones, a resident of El Cerrito, with a construction business located in Oakland, was the President of Trans-Bay Engineers and Builders and one time President of the National Association of Minority Contractors. In considering the plight of African Americans attempting to join a union, Mr. Dones stated that:

> The only way we could get work in certain trades—and electrical is an example, or sheetmetal workers or even plumbers—[was] to go out and get yourself a license and bid on a job and get it as an entrepreneur, when you could not make a living without having to fight a whole union bureaucracy as a craftsman.[11]

It was a long-standing fact that, in private work, organized labor virtually excluded African Americans from the electrical, plumbing/pipefitting and sheetmetal trades until well into the 1960s and sometimes beyond. The reality of what was happening on Mare Island was a reflection of that fact. Jake Sloan, who, by the time of the group interview in 2003, had written a MA thesis partly dealing with the situation in the building trades, said, "Well, on the outside [the private sector] in the building trades, the trades that were the hardest to get into for blacks, were the electrical, sheet metal, and pipe trades."[12]

African American participation in the building trades in the San Francisco-Oakland Bay Area, in general, during the period under consideration, can be determined from the census data for 1960. For example, in that year, there were known to be 5,461 plumbers/pipefitters in the area. Of those, 140 or 2 percent were non-white. Eighty-seven were African Americans.[13] Most of them were probably federally employed at either the Hunters Point or Mare Island Naval Shipyards. Many of those workers had been employed in the naval shipyards since World War II, when there was a labor shortage in all trades. Also, many classified as pipefitters were actually pipefitter helpers. Discrimination in the building trades was real and extreme, especially in the skill crafts. If not for the government jobs, there would have been virtually no African American plumbers/pipefitters in the whole area. In reality, off the shipyards, there was no opportunity for African Americans and other minority group members. Many of the men who eventually signed the complaint worked as pipefitter helpers, limited mechanics or mechanics. Then, and for many years to come, for Willie Long and the others in Shop 56, for employment opportunities, it was Mare Island, Hunters Point or nowhere. Is it any wonder that Jim Davis was ecstatic at becoming an apprentice and then a journeyman pipefitter at Mare Island in 1956?

***

Clearly, in the minds of some, it was time for some aggressive action. There really was no alternative, save living with the status quo. There was nowhere to go. Led by Willie Long, some of the African American workers at Mare Island were ready to move.

As they prepared to move, Willie Long and the others recognized what they were getting into. Before 1961, as mentioned above, other attempts to address the discrimination at Mare Island had all failed and sometimes resulted in very negative results. According to Boston Banks, "Yes, people got fired because they wanted to organize. That was the reason that [when] the 21er group came together...we were meeting in basements, because had they known that we were trying to form an organization to fight this, they would have fired every one of us."[14] Also, as mentioned before, and it was very clearly remembered by some of the men, John Edmondson was involved in at least one earlier failed attempt. According to Jim Davis,

> John had been involved with an earlier...attempt to fight discrimination and a group of blacks and everyone had backed out but him and this guy [Daryl] Franklin. There was mass layoffs, [people] got fired and various things. And that's why John wouldn't sign the second time, cuz he didn't think, he said, the blacks weren't going to stick together. That was his thing, cuz his experience had dictated. He would help us financially, but he wasn't going to sign anything, you know.[15]

With that in mind by all, secrecy was critical and yet difficult. In the March 2003 interview, Sloan wanted to know how the organizing was kept a secret, because many African Americans on Mare Island were afraid and known to be "snitches," those who could not be trusted to not divulge everything to the white leadership. When Sloan asked how everything had been kept "under wraps," Boston Banks' answered, "... handpicked people. That's, that's the way it was. Like I said, I didn't even talk to the machinist, the black machinist that I knew in my shop. He was a type of person that would come back and sit down in a group of whites and tell them all about everything."[16]

The case for action had been building. As noted above, some workers, men such as Louis Greer, had actually made official, written complaints before the 21er complaint was filed. Even as late as early 1961, Greer had filed a complaint of discrimination, claiming that unwarranted action had led to discipline. In one complaint he stated:

> It is my belief that I can establish a "PRIMA FACIE CASE regarding the issues of racial prejudice. I am of colored origin and it is known that our [Paint Shop] Master dislikes members of my race, and that information supporting this can be provided by the Industrial Relations Branch at Mare Island showing that nearly 100% of the disciplinary actions in the last five years were against employees of non-Caucasian origin.[17]

Having already lost faith in the leadership at Mare Island, Greer sent the complaint to John Connally, then Secretary of the Navy in the Kennedy administration.

As far as is currently known, a total of six formal complaints were filed from the mid-1950s to the time the 21er complaint was filed in November 1961. No action was taken; the complaints led to nothing. Long and some of his eventual followers were well aware of the past failures to organize and maintain unity, but he and the others were undeterred.

The stars were aligning, even to the extent that some of those who joined were aware at the time that there were independence movements taking place in Africa, the Middle East and Asia. Those movements were sometimes part of the discussions during the carpooling drives to and from Mare Island. The independence movement may have influenced some of them. This was certainly true of Fluker and Sloan. "Charlie Fluker certainly talked about it," said Jake Sloan.[18]

ORGANIZING: THE PLAYERS

Unlike the other civil rights activities at the time, the 21er actions and movement would be almost strictly grass roots driven and managed. Although there were many, the local churches were not directly involved, the local branch of the NAACP in Vallejo was not involved, and the academics in the area, the few that there were at the time, were not involved. With the exception of their attorney, Charles Wilson, most of the men had no college education and none had an undergraduate degree. A look at the key players will show that they were strictly blue collar workers, with no real political or economic connections or network to depend upon, except indirectly through their attorney, Charles Wilson, and his connections with the NAACP, the Men of Tomorrow, and the East Bay Democratic Club. Ultimately, this may have been to their advantage, because, often, especially at that time, the "leadership" of African American groups was chosen by people other than themselves.

And so, the past failed complaints and attempts to organize notwithstanding, and encouraged by what was happening in the Civil Rights Movement, both in the South and in the Bay Area, some African Americans on Mare Island were ready to take direct action. One of the driving forces of the process, even though he did not participate directly, was John Edmondson, at least at the strategic and inspirational levels and, above all, in the mind of Willie Long. In an indirect sense, Edmondson may have had more influence over the creation of the Original 21-25 than Willie Long. "If anybody in Shop 56 deserved to be a supervisor it should have been John Edmondson," according to Willie Long.[19] The fact that Edmondson was never promoted was deeply resented by those who admired and respected him, most especially by Willie Long. Others felt the same way. More than two decades after John died in 1979, when asked who had most influenced him, Jim Davis would say:

> Of course, one of them was John Edmondson, because he personified that not only was you as good as everyone, but you were better than

most. I kind of latched on to that. And, of course, Fluker, who was very smooth in his approach to things. Of course, Willie never gave up. That's the thing. But John gave you that pride. John, [with] all the shit he went through.[20]

Although he was recruited by Willie Long and Charles Fluker, two men that he respected, as the Original 21er group was being formed, Edmondson refused to join, thinking that the African Americans would eventually turn on each other, the way they had before. However, although he did not join, he gave financial support and advice to the group.

Naturally, Edmondson had some impact on the thinking of Long, because they worked in the same shop, and belonged to the same Masonic Lodge, according to John's daughter, Catherine. They knew each other well. John was an influence in both his daily work and philosophy and in Long's personal life. For example, he had advised Long during a difficult divorce. Even more than others, Long was angry that Edmondson had been "passed over, around and all those things." He promised him, "John-if I can get in a position where I can- I will do some of the things you were trying to do."[21] Many others felt the same way about Edmondson. In the thinking of Jake Sloan, "Whenever I would see John, I would think of strong men like Jackie Robinson. Later, once I got to know his story and saw photos of him, Frederick Douglass, the great abolitionist and social reformer, would come to mind when thinking of John. Strong. Proud."[22]

***

With all this as background, enter Willie Long, who had, in some sense, been waiting in the wings for a long time, at least a decade or more. Edmondson may have been the spirit and inspiration behind the organizing, but the driving force, the unquestioned leader was Willie Long. Born in 1918, in Jenkinsburg, Georgia, when Long was very young, his family moved to Atlanta, where his father worked as a construction laborer. At an early age, Long decided that he wanted to get out of "the category of just being a common laborer." In 1961, Long was a man who was well spoken and articulate. In talking with him, except in a few instances, one would never know that he had grown up in the South. Although he did not go to a college or university, he had studied extensively. He told the writer that his mother had always pushed him "to be something," although his family "was low class," according to him. [23] (He probably meant to say lower class. "Low class" is considered to be derogatory in African American society and Long would never have deliberately spoken of himself or his family in derogatory terms).

In 1947, Long started working at Mare Island as an apprentice pipefitter. For many reasons, personal and general, by 1960, he had become completely dissatisfied with working conditions and lack of fair training, promotional opportunities and pay for African Americans working at The Shipyard. In late 1960 and early 1961, by then 42 years old, he felt it was time to organize a protest. He became more committed after he heard that President John Kennedy had said, in so many words, that anyone who felt discriminated against should speak up, although he had been thinking about doing something for at least a decade. He was also inspired by what he was reading about on events developing and evolving in the South, in addition to events taking place in the Bay Area. Since the mid-1950s, he and others on Mare Island had been reading about African Americans in the South who were literally putting their lives on the line for freedom and equality. The Freedom Riders and the violent actions taken against them certainly had an impact on Long. To quote him, based on an interview conducted in 1980, "I said, if those people, in the South, can give up their lives for what they believe in, then I can put this little job on the line."[24] Others were also deeply affected. "I wanted to do something," said Jake Sloan, "but I did not want to go down South and get my head cracked."[25] As a resident of Oakland, Long was also informed and inspired by what was happening with local activists, in addition to what was happening in the South.

Before coming to work at Mare Island, Long had worked at naval shipyards in South Carolina and New Jersey. Although he could have gotten a deferment, he had earlier served in the Navy for 2 years as an aviation machinist's mate, living in segregated barracks, after having entered the service in 1943. At the time, he had seen most African American working mainly as mess men, which distressed him. After leaving the Navy and then working on the East Coast for a while, Long took several exams to become an apprentice. In 1947, he passed one to become an aviation machinist at Alameda Naval Air Station, near his home in Oakland. He also took the exam to become an apprentice pipefitter at Mare Island. He passed the exam and then decided to work at The Shipyard. When he started, he made 62 cents an hour, after quitting a job that paid $1.10. According to Long, a total of sixteen African Americans were in his apprentice class. He was the only one who finished. The others dropped out, because of the tremendous pressure, low wages and discrimination, said Long. As told by Long, when he completed the program, he was given his certificate with little comment from Erwin Whitthorne, the Shop Master, whereas, "when the gray [white] boys finished, they met in a conference room and were told you have accomplished this, you have accomplished that..."[26] Long points to John Edmondson as a huge, positive influence on him at the time, as was Charlie Fluker. "Almost every apprentice who went through until 1962 was influenced by John," said Long. He went on to say that John told him, "If it's something in the apprenticeship for these gray boys, there is something in it for you. Stick with it."[27] After he made the decision to hang in, Long was so dedicated that when they shortened the schooling for the sake of efficiency, "I cried. I wanted that extra schooling that I was not getting."[28] He was a man who was absolutely committed to excellence but also a man who wanted to be treated fairly in training and promotional opportunities. And he wanted John Edmondson and others to be treated fairly, as well.

At the time of the action, and for many years afterward, Sloan thought that Long was putting everything he had worked for at risk, but, in fact, Long had made a calculation, which he would divulge in the interview in 1980. "When I,-I should say we-started this thing, I had 20 years of service [including military and other governmental work time]. At the time, they said that if you had 20 years of service, without any problems, with a good record, before they could fire you they would have to retire you. So I took that as leverage." This was in 1961, but "I had been thinking about it since 1951"[29]. Long told Sloan that, "we started whispering about what was happening and talking while car-pooling," from Oakland and Berkeley. "I had 4 guys riding [car-pooling] with me who had been denied the privilege of being paid for supervisory work. There was one guy who was always in charge but he never got paid for it. His name was [Levi] Jones." Two of Long's riders, Jones and Thomas King, would later sign the complaint. They were taking a huge risk but, as Long went on to say, "the element of surprise is what got us as far as we went."[30]

Beginning sometime in late 1960 or early 1961, Long took the lead in the organizing of what would become a relatively small group of African Americans to protest discriminatory practices in hiring, training, promotions and pay at Mare Island. As we have seen, at least on the part of Long and some others, the desire to protest had been growing for some time, since at least the late 1940s. Such men as John Edmondson and Charlie Fluker had somewhat quietly seethed over the mistreatment of African Americans for many years before 1961. Louis Greer also seethed and not so quietly. Edmondson was not always quietly seething, either. In fact, at several times in the late 1940s and 1950s, according to Willie Long and James Davis, Edmondson had tried to stage a protest, as described above. These experiences left Edmondson bitter over what he saw as a weakness of will among the African American workers on Mare Island, a bitterness that may have influenced his habit of, more often than not, having lunch alone. This time, however, past failures aside, Long led several organizing and strategy meetings at the homes of various participants, on a revolving basis, apparently starting with several meetings at the Vallejo home of Ruben Terrell, a pipefitter working in Shop 56. The purpose was to organize a group to confront, head-on, the variety of discriminatory practices against African American workers at Mare Island.

***

Among the organizers who became leaders, there was a range of personalities and temperaments. Willie Long and Brodie Taylor were the fiery revolutionaries, prepared to do anything to further the cause. Boston Banks, Matt Barnes, and Eddie Brady seem to have been the moderating voices and forces in the leadership of the group, although Banks could be extremely forceful and outspoken at times. Jim Davis was seen by some, especially by Edmondson and some of the later white sympathizers, as a little sharp in his attitude, but no one could question his complete commitment. Willie Capers, totally committed, although almost completely unlettered and inarticulate, would not back down or "take low" to any man. Clarence Williams was calm and very determined once he made the decision to join. Charles Fluker and Louis Greer were calm, cool and collected but adamant in their belief that there was rampant discrimination and that something had to be done about it. All had their roles to play. Most of the men who joined and signed, men such as Jake Sloan, took no leadership roles. Sloan, for example, was basically along because he believed in the Civil Rights Movement and in the leadership of the 21ers, particularly the leadership of Long, Taylor, Davis and Fluker, along with the-behind-the scenes role of Edmondson, one of his enduring heroes. As he said later, he was "basically being carried along by history."[31] The range of personalities and temperaments played an important role in the formation, evolution, focus and leadership of the organization, sometimes played out with sad personal and human outcomes. Thus, although Willie Long was the driving force in the organizing and start-up of the organization, everyone had a role to play and some were very influential men with strong personalities of their own, personalities that, eventually, led to internal strife. Some of the men who joined looked at the big picture and took the long view. Clarence Williams says that "Brodie [Taylor] always said we must do it and do it now, or it would just back up on the next generation. We must stop this now."[32] In some ways, they were determined to get into and cement their place in the middle class and see their children get the education and other opportunities denied them. Long, of course, was always about immediate and quantifiable results, although his actions would pay long-term benefits that he probably could not have foreseen at the time.

On the whole, it was a diverse group, but, mainly, conservative in social values. Many of the members were decidedly of a middle class, bourgeois mentally, attending church and frowning on drinking and drug use. Some were not. For example, Willie Capers, Jimmie James and Jake Sloan were more "street" oriented. James and Capers drank but did not use drugs. Sloan drank and, with the exception of heroin, used every drug available to him at the time. Some, like Fluker, Davis and Brady were "tweeners." They attended church and were somewhat conservative, but they were also attracted to the tamer elements of café society and would drink a little on occasion. They liked places like Slim Jenkins's Metropolitan Supper Club in West Oakland, places that were at least a step or two up from the "Juke Joints," places where they would sometimes come into contact with the sleeping car porters, members of the East

Bay Democratic Club, Men of Tomorrow and other socially and politically active individuals and organizations. Such night clubs were also attended by the more sophisticated pimps, gamblers and gangsters. Davis loved music and would attend such events as Duke Ellington concerts with Sloan, along with an occasional visit to a "Juke Joint," as did Fluker. Although he loved music, and was a good singer, Willie Long, along with some of the others, men such as Clarence Williams and Matt Barnes, would not have been "caught dead" in some of the places that Sloan, James and Capers would patronize in North Richmond and West Oakland. Sloan would not have been "caught dead" in a church, unless in a wedding, a funeral or on the trail of a woman. One of Clarence Williams' brothers was one of the toughest guys in Richmond, but that was not Williams' orientation. Although he could be tough, he was a Christian and a family man, as was Matt Barnes and most of the others. Some of the members were ladies men, even some of the married Christians. Some of the Original 21ers were quiet and kept to themselves, but Boston Banks, Jr. spoke-out--loudly. Banks stated that he could not march with Martin Luther King Jr., because Dr. King was a passive person; Banks insisted that if someone were to spit on him, he would spit back. Banks also stated that many times he did what he wanted to do, and would not live under the conditions of others. It may be of interest to note that all the men originally involved were born in the Southern United States. In most cases, aside from those who came on their own, their families brought them to California as they were seeking employment and other opportunities. They were part of the Second Great Migration that carried millions of African Americans out of the South.

***

In 2003, most of the surviving members of the 21es met at the Richmond home of Matt Barnes. A look at some of the men who were still alive and at the meeting, as well as a few who had passed away, represents a fairly broad reflection of some specifics of the rather broad range of individual personalities, backgrounds, and interests of some of those who would become Original 21ers. Most of them had played leadership roles from the time the complaint was filed and the years of highest activity after the filing. Present at the meeting were

Boston banks, Matt Barnes, Eddie Brady, Willie Capers, James Davis, Jake Sloan and Clarence Williams. Although still alive, Louis Greer was not at the meeting. With the exception of Sloan, all these men, although led by Willie Long, at some point, took a leadership role in what became the Original 21ers.

Boston Banks, Jr. was born in 1921 in Bowman, Oklahoma. From 1940 to 1942, Banks attended Tuskegee Institute in Alabama. There, he studied in the veterinary school, once considered the best in the world, and also did some work under the great scientist George Washington Carver. He wanted to be a Tuskegee Airman, but he was too tall, plus he had a hernia. Instead, he joined the Navy and became a motor machinist, at a time when most African Americans served as mess men, working in the roles of serving food and cleaning tables in dining quarters. Banks served in the South Pacific for three years, assigned first to a minesweeper, dragging cables to find mines, and then moved on to serving on a landing craft. After his military service, Banks took a job digging ditches and installing storm systems in the South Bay area in the San Francisco Bay area. He earned $2.25 per hour but felt he would have better opportunities and security at Mare Island, even though, at first, he had to take a large pay cut to start as an apprentice machinist.

At Mare Island, Banks, after training and working as an apprentice, became an Inside Machinist in Shop 31. At that time, he was the only African-American out of about 1,100 people in the shop. In 1961, because he had by then worked at The Shipyard for 11 years, and with no promotions in sight, Banks did not hesitate to take the step to sign the complaint of racial discrimination, even though, by then, he had five children to care for. Eventually, he worked at Mare Island for 38 years. According to Clarence Williams, Banks, obviously an outstanding individual, was one of the "driving forces" behind the 21ers' actions. He was initially the vice president the 21ers under president Willie Long and later became the President, when Long left the organization and employment at Mare island.

Later in life, Banks also ran an employment agency out of his home and helped African Americans seeking work. He helped African Americans find employment with Pacific Telephone Company and Pacific Gas & Electric, with various banks and in other service positions. He was also Vallejo's first Boy Scout master to accept African American children.

Matthew "Matt" Barnes was born in 1933, in Homer, Louisiana. His family migrated to California in 1947. He began working at Mare Island in Shop 38, the Outside Machine Shop, in 1951, soon after he graduated from Richmond Union High School. He was the first African American apprentice in the history of the shop. Matt was always the diplomat "and he made speeches almost every time we went to the hill," Said Williams, who went on to say that "Willie [Long] did not mince words. Matt said the same thing but more diplomatically."[33] Bruce Christensen, a Caucasian whose father worked with Barnes, and who later interacted with Barnes himself, says now that "I can echo Clarence's comment, because I worked with Matt and he always dealt with other Shipyard shops and departments in a diplomatic, professional manner, which was not always easy to do."[34] After his experience with the Original 21ers, Barnes later served on the National Board of Directors of the NAACP.

Eddie Brady was born in 1918, in Tallulah, Louisiana. He first began working at Mare Island in 1944, after leaving service in the Navy and working a short while in Los Angeles. He was trained as a mechanic, working in Shop 31, the Inside Machine Shop. To further his capacity, while working at Mare Island, he went to school in Vallejo Adult School, taking four hours of academic training and four hours of mechanical training. At one point in his career there was a Reduction in Force (RIF) action initiated at Mare Island, a process whereby specific shops were required to reduce workforce to the level of real needs. Based on seniority, with preference to veterans, affected workers could be transferred to other shops or departments where there was a manpower shortage. Brady was transferred to Supply and stayed there until the 21er complaint was filed, after which he then became a mechanic again and eventually became a supervisor in Shop 31.

Willie Capers was born in 1919 in Caddo Parish, Louisiana. After serving as a stevedore in World War II, when he learned the rigging trade, he began working as a laborer's helper at Mare Island in Shop 72. Although an extremely forceful personality, and fearless, Capers was the least articulate of the group, but he was passionately committed to the cause. More than 40 years after the complaint was filed, he would say that "for my part, I wanted to join to break down Mare Island, because it was prejudice for the blacks who couldn't get to a one paint society out of all them colors we had working out there. Naw, it was a sad story."[35] Not long after the filing of the complaint, Capers retired on disability.

James "Jim" Davis was born in 1933 in Morganza, Louisiana. When he was eleven years old, his family moved to Vallejo, where his father worked as a construction laborer. Early on, Jim showed himself to be an excellent all-around athlete, excelling in basketball, football, baseball and track. In high school, he was considered by many to be the best high jumper in Northern California, tying the Vallejo High School record by leaping 6 feet 4 inches. In 1952, he began working at Mare Island in Shop 56, entering into the pipefitter apprenticeship program, which he completed in 1956. During this time and later he continued to play semi-pro baseball and basketball, doing so until 1965. In 1961, at the time the complaint was filed, he was working as a journeyman pipefitter, working mainly on the construction of nuclear submarines. Sloan was his helper at the time. In 2014 Davis was elected to the Vallejo Athletic Hall of Fame.

Although he was not at the meeting that day in 2003, Louis Greer, who played an important role in the beginning with the group, was still alive and active. Greer was born in 1922, in Point, Texas. Like several others, he had served in the Army, attached to the Air Force, working in servicing planes. He moved to California in 1950. He then started work in Shop 71 as a painter, a trade that he had learned on-the-job before leaving Texas. One of the only one of those who became a 21er who had formally filed his own complaints, by 1960, Greer had many long-standing complaints of discrimination in his shop and was one of the first to begin organizing with Long, along with Charlie Fluker. Although he served on the shop committee, which reviewed various kinds of complaints, he told Sloan that African Americans in his shop were warned that they would lose their jobs for talking with him or Long. He left employment at Mare Island on a disability settlement. He had long owned jewelry and watch repair shop and so he then began to manage it full time, while, at the same time, investing in real estate and other business interests. Through these endeavors, he became a fairly wealthy man.

Jake Sloan was born in 1940 on a farm near the village of Tulip, Arkansas. His family migrated to California in 1948. In 1956, at the age of 15, he began dropping out of high school to serve on active duty in the California Army National Guard, which he had joined in March of that year. Then, in September, 1957, on his seventeenth birthday, he joined the regular Army. In July, 1960, upon being honorably discharged from the Army, he began working at Mare Island as a pipefitter's helper. Working at Mare Island was something of a tradition in Jake's family. His father and two of his uncles had worked there before he was hired. Sloan was not really in the group seeking personal promotions, although, after the filing, he did get a relatively fast promotion to the rate of pipefitter limited. Given his background and lack of a good basic education, Sloan could not have gotten a better job than the one he held at Mare Island at the time of the filing and he knew it.

Clarence Williams was born in 1933, El Dorado, Arkansas.1933. His family moved to California in 1940. His father built two apartment buildings on Sanford Avenue in North Richmond and the family lived in one. Almost by any standard, Clarence was a unique individual in his environment. As a boy, he had been very studious and industrious. In talking about his work, he said, "I was fascinated with nuclear physics and energy. That was the part that fascinated me most."[36] After high school, he first went to Contra Costa College in San Pablo, studied some engineering and then began working at Mare Island in Shop 11 in 1952. He worked as a helper, then limited mechanic and finally journeyman mechanic. He also worked in the main shipfitter office as a shop planner, although he was not paid at the rate of shop planner for the work. Like his father before him, in his free time, Williams built an apartment building and his family still lives in one of the units.

Of those 21ers men who had died by 2003, beyond Long, not much in detail is remembered about most of them. However, Charles Fluker and Brodie Taylor made an impression on everyone. This was particularly true of Fluker, who had died several years earlier. Taylor had died at a relatively young age many years before 2003. Fluker stood out in many ways. According to Williams, Fluker, who was Edmondson's brother-in-law at one time, was "very astute, sophisticated, well educated, used correct English all the time. He was the gentleman. Very intelligent gentleman and he was a force behind it [the filing], also. A wonderful, humane person."[37] Jake Sloan remembers that Fluker, although a fairly close friend, was much older than he and some of the others at the time. He was the one who, along with Long, had influenced him to join, although, at first, they were opposed to him doing so. In many ways, Fluker was a mentor to Sloan and to some of the other, younger men. Jim Davis recalled that Fluker, who died in the early 1990s, was close to 50 years old in 1961. Of Fluker, Davis would say that:

> Once he got involved, he was totally committed...like he was involved with the NAACP in Richmond. And he was one of the best member-ship guys ever. Fluker kept at you...and you can't get pissed off. He never changed his...you could argue with him all day, but when the sun go down, his point of view was still his point of view.[38]

Apparently, at his age, Fluker was not really in it for himself. When Sloan reminded everyone that Fluker, like Jim Davis, was well liked, especially by Witthorne, Jim Davis said, "Fluker used to tell, say that, he was involved for the young bucks. That's what he used to call us."[39]

Fluker's influence on some of the men went far beyond Mare Island and the discrimination that they faced there. For Davis and Sloan, Fluker was a friend and mentor who taught them how to deal with the general challenges of life, and, in particular, how to get along with women. Says Sloan, "I mean, I was 20 years old and Fluker was close to 50 and we'd go hang out. You know, Slim Jenkins [nightclub]."[40] Moreover, Fluker encouraged Sloan and other "young bucks" to get an education so that they would not be trapped working at Mare Island. Sloan heard and listened to him.

Although he was colorful, to say the least, and even though he was a fairly close friend of Sloan at the time, not much is remembered about Jimmie James, who worked as a helper for many years in Shop 56 and was a fairly strong voice in the group. What is remembered is a boast that he once made to Davis and Sloan. He claimed that, while he was serving in the armed forces in the Philippines, he had had sex with 200,000 women. When asked by Davis if he would settle with a claim of 100,000, he refused. James was colorful, adding to the interesting mix of personalities in the group. Colorful though he may have been, although James had worked at Mare Island for more than a decade at the time of the filing of the complaint, he was still serving as a helper.

The legal advisor for the group was Charles Wilson, an African American attorney, who was selected to draw-up the complaint, and provide legal advice and representation. Originally, there was another lawyer involved by the name of Fouche, who was from San Francisco, but, for reasons not remembered by the surviving members, the group had more confidence in Wilson, who was living in Berkeley at the time. Wilson's qualifications, preparation, and commitment could not be questioned. Born in Norfolk Virginia, Wilson graduated with honors, with a degree in economics, from Virginia Union University. He served four years in the Army during World War II, reaching the rank of first lieutenant. He then attended and graduated from Columbia University Law School in New York. When he agreed to work with the 21ers, he had been in law practice for more than 10 years. In later years, he was named as an administrative law judge for the State of California. At the time, he was an active member of the NAACP, which could have influenced his thinking, because, at least at the national level, the NAACP had been taking critical action to integrate the building trades since 1958. He was also a member of the influential East Bay Democratic Club and Men of Tomorrow in Oakland. The fact is that groups like the 21ers, which did not have the advantage of a highly educated leadership, could not get the kind of support that organizations like the NAACP or the Urban League could. The 21ers basically had to work alone, with Wilson as their main professional advocate. They were fortunate to get him. However, part of the strength of the 21ers was that the leadership could not be coopted by "the system," as, some people at the time considered to be the case with such people as Whitney Young of the Urban League. Many people are aware of the story of Thurgood Marshall, but many unknown African American lawyers played very important roles in gaining civil rights and equal employment opportunity, the bread and butter issues. One such lawyer was Charles Wilson. Kenneth W. Mack, Professor of Law at Harvard Law School points out in *Representing the Race: The Creation of the Civil Rights Lawyer*, "Theirs is a different story and deserves to be told on its own terms."[41] As Howard Zinn has pointed out in his works, history is often created by many people who are seldom written about or recognized. Wilson was such a person.

Given this set of individuals, some with very strong personalities and viewpoints, the "bottom line" is that, although he was the unquestioned leader, at least in the beginning, Willie Long could not and did not do it alone. (For a complete list of all the men who signed the complaint, see appendix 2.)

ORGANIZING: THE CHALLENGES

"There comes a time when the cup of endurance runs over, and men are no longer willing to be plunged into an abyss of injustice where they experience the blackness of corroding despair." ~Martin Luther King. *Letter from a Birmingham Jail.*

The organizing was tough, very tough. When thinking back on organizing some of the African Americans, Clarence Williams remembers that, "When you started talking about complaining to the government, they [the African American workers] got away from you, because that [working at Mare Island] was actually a very good job. For blacks, civil service was a good, safe job, because it was harder to fire you." He went on to say, "... he [the worker] had a check every week. You could plan your lifestyle on that. They did not want to lose that and I could understand that."[42] This was particularly important because of union control of private work off The Island, given that the unions were largely antagonistic to African American membership. There were few opportunities for steady employment outside Mare Island or Hunters Point in San Francisco. Both before and after the filing, the organizing was also sometimes difficult at the personal level, said Eddie Brady:

> Mister Clarence Williams and I had the most embarrassing experience of all those [on the] shipyard. We were having lunch in the South Cafeteria and three blacks said we [were a] stupid, idiot group and called us dirty names and the president, Mr. Williams, just lost it almost. I had to cool him down.... [Members of Shop] 72 said we were getting plenty of overtime. We said we wanted more per hour and less overtime, so it was really a very few that would sign their name to anything.[43]

In any case, they had to be careful about those who were talked to at all in attempting to organize. There was a lot of precedent for this type of thinking and action. For example, while he was in prison, after his conversion to what he thought was Islam, Malcolm X started proselytizing among his African American fellow inmates. However, because of what he was preaching about whites at the time, he had to be careful: "I never knew when some brainwashed black imp, some dyed-in-the-wool Uncle Tom would nod at me and then go running to tell the white man."[44] The organizers at Mare Island had the same challenge. Asked how they were able to keep the organizing a secret, Williams paused and then said,

> Of necessity. No one really wanted to lose their job, especially the younger group. We had families like everybody else. It was a very good job to have. We did not want to jeopardize our family social and financial situation. Of necessity, we would kind of pick the people we would talk to. If they came right out and was against it, you would just let it go at that.[45]

According to all the survivors who were interviewed starting in 2003, usually, if they [the organizers] did not know a person, then they felt they could not trust them to not take the news back to [the leadership at] Mare Island. They weren't talked to. They weren't told anything about it. As far as those at that meeting in 2003 remembered it, the people invited to organizing meetings were carefully picked. There was great fear of being fired and people were only chosen if it was believed they would not say anything back on Mare Island during the day, because they all believed that they would have all been fired before the complaint could have gotten to Washington. According to Boston Banks,

> It was a matter of one on one, of the people that were there. I was talking to Davis. I would talk to Mr. Brady. We would talk to people that we felt we could trust that would show up at the meeting and back us that we, more or less, picked those people that we knew that wasn't going to go back and tell the shipyard what we were doing. It had to be closed. It couldn't be an open thing until that complaint [response] came back from Washington.[46]

When Willie Long, who took more chances than the others, talked with many of the African American workers, he was, more often than not, summarily rebuffed, but that was not the case when he talked with men such as

Boston Banks, who felt very strongly that he had been discriminated against since the beginning of his time at Mare Island and was anxious to do something about it. Banks felt that his maximum opportunity was to be a journeyman and he was not satisfied with that, even if his actions caused him to be fired. The same was true of Brady, Barnes, Davis, Fluker, Greer, Williams, Brody Taylor, and all the others who eventually joined the group and signed the complaint.

Beyond the fear of being fired, another reason that it was hard to organize the men was the fear of losing the opportunity to work overtime. Banks said that, "overtime was the overriding thing. A lot of the fellows that worked on Mare Island were earning more than their supervisor at the end of the year"[47,] because they were able to work a lot of overtime. Often, the men could work every weekend and seven days a week and were paid a premium for the extra hours. The problem was that, often, they had to work extra hours to make as much money as they would have on regular time if they had been treated fairly in promotions, recognition and pay for actual work performed.

Although very good and talented workers, the men of the group probably could not have found better jobs in the private sector, everything considered. To be taken into account for many, especially the veterans, were paid vacations, paid sick leave, health benefits, as well as a Civil Service retirement system for those who could achieve permanent status. And they were paid every week, without fail, which was not always the case in the private sector. The uneducated men like Capers, James and Sloan, all veterans, and permanent employees, certainly could not have gotten a more secure job elsewhere at the time. There were many, many others like them. None of this could be taken lightly, in attempting to organize.

***

As time went by, Edmondson was increasingly very concerned about the danger of the organizing, according to Jim Davis, "and I can remember John Edmondson saying, you guys are playing with fire, you know, cuz some of the same people you are trying to help, will turn you in."[48] Even after the filing, there was much fear and apprehension on the part of the African American workers, as remembered by Brady, "and I can recall, after we were organized and we could go up [to the main offices] and help people and go to meetings, blacks would see us going up and say, 'Well, I won't be seeing you next week. Naw, naw, you won't be here next week, you know."[49] They were repeatedly told by other African American workers that they were going to be fired. It should be understood and remembered that some of the men had come from living under a system of terror in the South. One of the major challenges for Long *et al* was to get the African American workers to overcome an underlying fear of confronting whites over basic issues of equality. Because of that fear and other very real issues of concern, they looked for all kinds of excuses to either not participate at all or to drop out after starting. For example, at one organizational meeting, a guy from the pipe shop named Blocker left, using the excuse that the organizers were not using Robert's Rules of Order to conduct the meeting. Be that as it may, amazingly, to his ever-lasting credit, neither Blocker, nor others, for that matter, as far as is known, disclosed the fact of the organizing once they were aware of it.

A form of group thinking and circumstance also had impacts on the organizers. In addition to the meetings, the fact that many of the men carpooled together probably made it easier for them to communicate and organize in relative secrecy. Also, many of the signers worked relatively closely together in shop 56, both in the shop and on ships and submarines. Willie Long, Jake Sloan, Jimmy James, Jim Davis, Charlie Fluker, Ruben Terrell, all signers, worked in the Pipe Shop, as did John Edmondson, Long's mentor, and Vernon Taylor, who joined soon after the first 25 signers. It may also be significant to note that, in addition to the fact that about a third of the signers worked in Shop 56, about a third lived in Richmond, which had been a hotbed of civil rights activism going back to the mid-1940s, driven by what was probably the most activist NAACP chapter on the West Coast. Fluker, Barnes, James, Williams and Sloan all belonged to the Richmond NAACP. Fluker was very active in the chapter, as was Barnes, who later became a national leader. In fact, membership in the NAACP was a kind of connecting factor. Several signers from Vallejo, including Boston Banks, were members. Willie Long was a member of the Oakland branch and attorney Wilson was a member of the

Berkeley branch. In those days, the NAACP was much more attractive to activists than it is today. The NAACP connection and influence ran through almost everything. As far as is known, at minimum, Fluker, Long, Sloan, James, Edmondson, Banks, Brady, Taylor, Williams, Greer, and Davis belonged to the organization. However, it should also be noted that the Vallejo chapter did not actively support the 21ers at any time after the filing.

A relatively very small number of African Americans eventually signed the complaint. One fairly notable person who did not join was George Livingston, who went on to become mayor of the City of Richmond. He was not alone, of course. The overwhelming number of the African Americans at Mare Island refused to sign and join the protest. One of Jake Sloan's uncles was working on The Shipyard at the time but adamantly refused to become signatory to the complaint. A veteran, he had a young family to support and could see no other means of equivalent employment or security off Mare Island. In addition, he would have known about Jake's father, a former worker at Mare Island, and a friend, who had once hitch-hiked from Richmond to the sawmills around McCloud, in the North of California, working on farms on the way up, living in hovels and being paid on a hard, race-tiered or piece- work basis once they got there. No one would want to trade a job at Mare Island for that. In recent years, when asked why they did not sign, some African Americans did not remember, others said such things as they knew nothing about it, which is very likely possible, in some cases, given the method of organizing.

At first, the younger men had been discouraged from joining the protest, but, ultimately, four of them signed. Later, interestingly enough, three of them became very influential in the organization and one, James Davis, in the 1970s, became the leader of the group. The youngest, Jake Sloan, never took any leadership role and had virtually no influence in the group during the years of activism.

Beyond the obvious and widespread discrimination, what also influenced Davis and Sloan to join and sign was their respect for certain leaders in Shop 56. As Davis said,

> Well, basically, a majority [of] guys [that] joined was from the pipe shop [Shop 56]. Hate to say that, but that's a fact. And, ah, the people that influenced me were John Edmondson and Charlie Fluker and

Willie Long, and those were basically the blacks that I was around and
they liked to talk, and, of course, you [Sloan] became a part of that
group.[50]

After all the years of facing blatant discrimination, and after months of
meetings and organizing, first 21 men and then, eventually, 25 were prepared
to take direct action at Mare Island. In reality, the momentum to do something
had been building for decades. The fact that John Edmonson was still a mechanic in 1961 was the tip of the iceberg of a monumental travesty played out
against the African Americans working at Mare Island. At the same time that
the lead organizers were still recruiting people, Willie Long and Charles Wilson, with input from some of the recruits, were drawing up a draft complaint.

Notes:

1. Barry Goldwater, with Jack Casserly. *Goldwater*. (New York: Doubleday, 1988), p. 108.

2. Juan Williams, *Thurgood Marshall: American Revolutionary*. (New York: Times Books, 1998), p. 308.

3. Nick Bryant, *The Bystander: John F. Kennedy and the Struggle for Black Equality*. (New York: Basic Books, 2006), p. 218.

4. Jake Sloan, *Foundations for a Quiet Rebel*. Unpublished paper.

5. Leonard Pitts, *Conservatives Long for Days of Yesteryear*. Bay Area News Group, November 5, 2012, p. 7.

6. Thomas Peele, *Killing the Messenger: The Story of Radical Faith, Racism's Backlash, and the Assassination of a Journalist*. (New York: Crown Publishers, 2012), p. 141.

7. Shirley Ann Wilson-Moore, *To Place These Deeds. The African American Community in Richmond, California 1910-1963*. (Berkeley: University of California Press, 2000), p. 70.

8. Ibid., p. 165.

9. Robert O. Self, *American Babylon: Race and the Struggle for Postwar Oakland*. (Princeton: Princeton Univ. Press, 2003), p. 12.

10. Marshall, *Op. Cit.,* p. 64.

11. Ray Dones, in recorded interview by Jake Sloan. November 7, 1979, Oakland, California.

12. Boston Banks, Matthew Barnes, Eddie Brady, Willie Capers, James Davis, Jake Sloan, Clarence Williams, in recorded interview by Jake Sloan. March 22, 2003, Richmond, California.

13. US Department of Commerce, Bureau of Census, United States Census of Population: 1960, VOL 1, Characteristics of Population, Pt 6 Sec 2, California.

14. *Vallejo Times Herald*, November 12, 2006, p. A3.

15. Boston Banks, Barnes, *et al* interview.

16. Ibid.

17. Louis Greer, Letter to John Connally, Secretary of the Navy, April 12, 1961.

18. Jake Sloan, *Notes and Reminiscences, op. cit.*

19. Willie Long, in recorded interview by Jake Sloan. July 2, 1980, Madera, California.

20. Boston Banks and James Davis, in recorded interview by Jake Sloan. July 2, 2004, Vallejo, California.
21. Willie Long interview.
22. Jake Sloan, *Notes and Reminiscences, op. cit.*
23. Willie Long interview.
24. Ibid.
25. *Vallejo Times Herald.* February 18, 2007. p. A3.
26. Willie Long interview.
27. Ibid.
28. Ibid.
29. Ibid.
30. Ibid.
31. Jake Sloan Memorial Stone Speech, Alden Park, Mare Island, November 17, 2010.
32. Clarence Williams interview.
33. Ibid.
34. Bruce Christensen, Email to Jake Sloan. February 3, 2014.
35. Banks, Barnes, *et al* interview.
36. Clarence Williams interview
37. Ibid.
38. Banks, Davis interview.
39. Banks, Barnes, *et al* interview.
40. Ibid.
41. Kenneth W. Mack, *Representing the Race: The Creation of the Civil Rights Lawyer.* (Cambridge: Harvard Univ. Press, 2012), p. 69.
42. Clarence Williams interview
43. Banks, Barnes, *et al* interview.
44. Malcom X, *The Autobiography of Malcolm X*, as told to Alex Haley. (New York: Ballantine Books, 1965), p. 186.
45. Clarence Williams interview.
46. Banks, Barnes, *et al* interview.
47. Ibid.
48. Ibid.
49. Ibid.
50. Ibid.

CHAPTER 3

Filing the Complaint

Once formulated, the complaint needed signatures, as many as could be collected, which had been the primary goal of the organizing. Long, who later became the 21ers first official president, an action which took place some 2 years after the filing, continued working The Shipyard, seeking as many African American workers to join in the effort as possible. "He was going around The Shipyard, trying to recruit guys...[but] people were literally running away when he showed up," Sloan would say later.[1]

At the last minute, again, some of the older men tried to keep the younger men from signing the document and jeopardizing their fledgling careers, the surviving 21ers said in the 2003 interview. However, the four youngest, Matt Barnes, James Davis Jake Sloan and Clarence Williams, signed anyway, with some lingering reservations. "I didn't want to lose my job," Davis said, adding "I was a young man with a family." Despite their fears, all of the men knew it was time. "If not us, who?" Davis continued. "The confidence we had in each other exceeded the prejudice. We may be fired or put into a ditch, but we'll be in a ditch together," he concluded.[2] They felt that it was time to stand up and be counted. Said Williams, "We were young men who had families, and I didn't want my children to have to go through what we did."[3] They were ready to go. The fact that they could not get more signatures, Sloan recalled, "was amazing to us, because there were guys there [at Mare Island] that I was working with who clearly had been discriminated against. I mean, guys who were helpers for

15 to 20 years who wouldn't sign the thing. They tried to talk me out of signing it," Sloan said.[4] No luck.

Once the complaint was ready to go, they had to move fast. "We were definitely working against time...that element of surprise was what got us as far as we got," Long said. "Now, if we had waited two or three months after that first meeting, to get our signatures and send this letter off, then we would have been sunk," Long said. "We did it without Mare Island [management] knowing anything at all."[5] At the time, the 21ers didn't grasp the complaint's long-term significance. The fact that they could only get a total of 25 signatures dismayed and would continue to dismay Sloan for many years afterward. "There were probably thousands of African Americans working on the shipyard, but only the signers had nerve enough to do it," Sloan said.[6] (In recent years, Sloan has come to believe that, logistically, and realistically, it would have been nearly impossible to get very many more signatures and that, in the end, they got enough).

It had been hard, very hard but, after the months of secret meetings and organizing, the complaint was signed, with the first signing taking place one evening in November at Charles Fluker's home at 430 South 17th Street in Richmond. That evening, 21 men signed the complaint and then, over the next few days, another 4 were convinced to sign the document, which was officially filed on Friday, November 17, 1961. They felt strongly that they could not wait any longer.

Fundamentally, what drove the organizing was the utter unfairness of training, promotional, and equal pay opportunities. As stated in the complaint, "Conditions have reached such a sad state of affairs regarding discrimination against Negroes that we are forced to appeal to your committee [the PCEEO] for some kind of redress." The original complaint focused on nine areas:

1. The unwritten practices in not upgrading third step Negro mechanics (journeymen)
2. The systematic barring of Negroes from promotion to supervisor
3. The systematic practice of failing Negroes on the oral interview stage for promotion to supervisor
4. The lack of opportunity for Negroes to enter apprenticeship programs

5. The lack of recognition of Negroes in awarding of the Superior Accomplishment Awards

6. The lack of opportunity for Negroes to be trained for positions in the new field of Atomic [Nuclear] Shipbuilding

7. The discrimination against Negroes in post apprenticeship training opportunities

8. The discrimination against Negroes in job assignments

9. The failure to promote Negro helpers to the position of mechanic (journeyman), in some cases even after 15 years of experience (For details of the complaint, see Appendix 3.)

They did not know it when the complaint was filed, but the men-young and middle-aged, helpers, apprentices and journeymen- were, by filing the complaint, helping to lay some of the groundwork for possibly indirectly influencing the Civil Rights Act of 1964 and, directly, influencing early affirmative action approaches at Mare Island, in Vallejo, and other federal facilities throughout the country. It may have also influenced the possibility of unionization of civilians working for the military at Mare Island. At the time, all the men wanted was a wage comparable to that of their white co-workers for comparable work, and equal treatment in training and promotional opportunities. Eventually, what they got was a lot more, both for some of the signers and for many others, including some of the African Americans who refused to become signatory to the complaint and participate in the action. What they helped to start was a chain reaction that continues to be felt to this day and beyond, providing additional benefits and opportunities for themselves and many, many others, some of whom had refused to support the effort in the beginning and, indeed, some who had ridiculed it.

There were to be many problems to overcome in the coming years, but, over time, the action brought great changes at Mare Island and far beyond, in the areas of equal opportunity and affirmative action. The group that later became known as The Original 21ers has survived, in one form or another, to the present. The men still alive are still somewhat dismayed that only 25 African Americans would sign the complaint when there were hundreds, if not thousands, of them working at the shipyard under discriminatory conditions.

At the time, no one could have anticipated what the short or long-term impacts would be, how the federal government or the leadership at Mare Island would respond or how the 21ers would respond and evolve over the years. They soon began to find out. For one thing, the complaint would, over time, result in some of the desired results but would, also over time, reveal some deficiencies, some of which would prove to be important.

Notes:

1. *Vallejo Times Herald*, November 12, 2006, p. A3.
2. Ibid.
3. Ibid.
4. Ibid.
5. Willie Long interview.
6. *Vallejo Times Herald*, November 12, 20016, p.A3

CHAPTER 4

Follow Up: The Short and Mid-term Impacts, 1961-1964

Some 45 years after the filing of the complaint, an article in the *Vallejo Times-Herald* reported that "The complaint quickly helped to bring sweeping changes locally and nationally at military installations, including early affirmative action programs."[1] That was incorrect. Real change did come, but it would not come quickly, and it did not come without great, ongoing struggle and perseverance on the part of Willie Long and the other members of the 21ers. Ultimately, the goals of the 21ers were largely met, but not quickly, and not without a tremendous and continuing struggle that, in some ways, lasted from the time right after the filing in early 1962 until the closure of Mare Island in 1996.

The two men who served as shipyard commanders at Mare Island during the initial, and greatest, period of activism on the part of the 21ers, were Admirals Leroy V. Honsinger and Edward J. Fahey, both of whom had served in the segregated Navy of World War II and immediately afterward, at a time when African Americans mainly served as mess men in that branch of the military. Their view of African American men, then, would have been largely informed by the experience of viewing African Americans working in the role of serving food and cleaning tables in dining quarters, basically working as servants. This probably affected their general thinking towards African American workers, in general, and the 21ers, in particular. In fact, it may well have been that, until the reading of the complaint and listening to the complainants in person, neither of them had ever really thought of the then existing working conditions for African Americans as discriminatory. Generally speaking, at least among whites, Honsinger was known to be "a hard but fair taskmaster."[2] According to Bruce Christensen, whose father worked in Shop 38 at the time, Honsinger "was known as Admiral 'Gunslinger' because of the way he treated his employees (all races)."[3] He was known to be "hard-nosed" and appeared to take pride in the reputation.

After the complaint was mailed to the PCEEO, an article that appeared in a San Francisco newspaper, the old *News Call Bulletin,* gave it some attention, but nothing appeared in the local papers in Oakland, Richmond or Vallejo. That set a trend for a lack of even general knowledge of the 21ers and the plight of African Americans at Mare Island, a trend that would hold for many years to come.

In early December, 1961 the complaint was forwarded from the PCEEO back to Mare Island, which conducted a preliminary "investigation" and appraisal. On the issue of a finding of discrimination, this was the start of a long series of official Navy "runarounds" to be faced by the complainants, lasting over a period of several years.

The initial investigation was completed on January 8, 1962, with the finding that, on the issue of discrimination, "…investigation disclosed no substantiating evidence against the Shipyard."[4] Then, on January 17, a "negotiation" meeting was held to discuss the findings. In the meeting were Admiral Honsinger, along with the Deputy Employment Policy Officer, 21er attorney Wilson, and most of the 25 complainants. During the meeting, attorney Wilson presented two more complaints. After that meeting, Admiral Honsinger concluded that…"their allegations were based on a general feeling of frustration and lack of motivation."[5] There were no findings of discrimination.

At the request of attorney Wilson, and the complainants, there was a formal hearing held on March 1, 1962, with all the principals present, including Honsinger, as well as eight additional witnesses for the complainants. The additional complainants had been recruited by Willie Long, after the filing in November. Honsinger and The Shipyard leadership again reached the conclusion that the complaints were unsubstantiated. According to Honsinger's report,

On March 1st the group, and several more witnesses, were given an opportunity to express themselves more fully in a formal hearing. As a result, I arrived at two conclusions:

a. The specific allegations were not substantiated and there was no finding of a policy on discriminating practice on the Shipyard.

b. Nevertheless, a great deal of effort on the part of management personnel of the Shipyard will be required to overcome feelings of frustration on the part of the Group. Particular areas to be considered are promotion practices, rotation of tasks, additional pay assignments, broader training opportunities, and dissemination of information.[6]

In effect, his observations in (b) indicate an admission that virtually all the issues identified in the complaint were real and the result of racism, but were put at the foot of "frustration and lack of motivation." In the hearing, he said to the group that, going forward, he would make sure all Mare Island personnel understood the discrimination rules, whatever they were at the time. It was all thought to be a sham by the 21ers. For example, in defending yard practices, in one instance, it was even said that the reason that African Americans did not get promoted was because they didn't attend social events, as opposed to the fact of racism.

In spite of the fact that the leadership at Mare Island did not do any real investigation of the issues identified in the complaint, Willie Long continued to follow through with his activism. When Honsinger left, after essentially "passing the buck" or "kicking the can down the road" and Admiral Fahy became Shipyard Commander, in late March of 1962, Long and attorney Wilson started making attempts to talk with him. The Navy continued to support Honsinger's "findings." In May, 1962 Admiral Fahy, a Mr. Burke and a Mr. Briggs met with attorney Wilson in Admiral Fahy's office. There were no new developments reported out of the meeting.

In the ongoing cover-up, In June, 1962, the Navy Department Employment Policy Officer made a determination that no racial bias had been found, stating, in part, "After a careful review of the entire record I do not find evidence of racial bias in the incidents cited. I am also not convinced by the evidence that a pattern of discrimination exists."[7]

How could the Navy make such findings? One answer may be that there was a lack of statistical evidence supporting the complaint, allowing for "wiggle room" in the responses. None of the nine issues identified in the original complaint included supportive numbers. For example, the complaint did not point out that there was not a single African American supervisor in Shop 56 and that there were less than five on the whole shipyard. This may have emboldened the Navy to make such statements as: "While it has not been demonstrated that racial discrimination resulted in any improper action at the Shipyard, *the Deputy Employment Policy Officer has initiated vigorous action to correct the deficiencies.* [Emphasis added][8] There was no mention of the causes for the "deficiencies." Attorney Wilson then sent a letter to the PCEEO requesting a review of the decision.

Attorney Wilson made several attempts to schedule a meeting between Admiral Fahy, Willie Long and the other complainants in 1962. Fahy only agreed to meet alone with Wilson, finally agreeing to a meeting for December 27. For reasons unknown at this time, Wilson did not show-up for the meeting. It is not hard to imagine that by that time he felt that he was wasting his time, as a result of what had transpired after the filing on the complaint more than a year before the scheduled meeting.

The pattern continued in a similar vein of denial. In February, 1963, Fahy issued a memo that concluded, in part:

> An appraisal of local employment patterns, including use of statistical information gathered in the 1961 and 1962 "head counts', has given no indication of non-compliance with Executive Order 1095. ...Investigation disclosed no substantial proof of discrimination at the Shipyard but showed that the allegations were based on feelings of frustration and lack of motivation. Since that time, a considerable amount of effort on the part of management personnel has been applied to overcome those feelings.9

However, Admiral Fahy's conclusion notwithstanding, discriminatory practices were continuing. For example, on the old issues of "broken time" and hyper discrimination against African Americans in the skill crafts, in August of 1962, African American worker Edgar Dillion wrote a complaint letter to Fahy stating, in part, "...in the sheetmetal shop [17], comprised of nearly four hundred fifty employees now working there, there are only twenty-eight Negroes, and in my nearly eighteen months of work at this activity, I have never seen a Negro rehired."[10] It is not hard to imagine that a large majority of the twenty-eight were helpers. In fact, to further discredit Fahy's conclusion, in 1962, the year following the filing of the complaint, at least three other individual complaints filed with the Shipyard Commander were found to be lacking in proof, although, in at least one case, the Navy ultimately found otherwise.

With all this, the general forms of discrimination continued. According to Clarence Williams, Fahy was more sympathetic than Honsinger, but he remembers a meeting with him in which "he referred to us as boys." Williams told Fahey that the children of the 21ers "are at home" and that "there are no boys here."[11]

At first, the general response to the complaint was, at best, dismaying for the 21ers, and caused a great deal of concern for the men who had signed it. Matt Barnes claims that:

> The basic kind of response was, even though that commission [the PCEEO], they didn't find any racial discrimination, but found that there were some mis...what you call it...mismanagement kind of practices that were wrong. They would not say, in response to the complaint, would not say that there were practices of racial discrimination, but [that there] was some mismanagement kind of problems that the shipyard had.[12]

The response from President Kennedy's PCEEO was also being slowly drawn-out. Led by vice president Lyndon Johnson, it was apparently increasingly getting similar complaints from across the country. More than a year after the complaint was filed, the PCEEO communicated to Long that it would review the complaint, but was backlogged due to the increasing number of complaints and appeals coming in for its attention. After some follow-up correspondence complaining of lack of progress at Mare Island, in March, 1963, Long received a letter informing him that "We have not had an opportunity yet to review your complaint inasmuch as there are a number of cases still ahead of yours on our docket."[13]

The runaround on a finding of discrimination continued, in various forms, for many months. Finally, in September, 1963, the PCEEO delegated a review team/committee to visit several installations in the Bay Area, one of which was Mare Island. Almost a full two years after the filing, in October of 1963, the committee visited The Shipyard for three days to make an "investigation" of issues of equal employment and promotions. The purpose of the visit could not have been serious. In face of the fact that there had been a specific complaint filed almost 2 years earlier, the chairperson of the committee, Joseph A Cirilo, stated that "Allegations of past discrimination will not be entertained and no individuals will be interviewed." Going on, according to Cirilo, "The team's mission is to devise ways and means of utilizing the resources of minority groups in the naval activities to the fullest extent possible, insofar as governing Civil Service rules and regulations." Somehow, this was to be accomplished by surveying "records, recruitment methods and sources, merit promotion plans and similar programs now in operation."[14]

It is difficult to imagine what they could have found. In January of that same year, Admiral Fahy had laid out his 10 goals for the year, as published in the January issue of the shipyard newspaper, *The Grapevine*.[15] There was no mention of equal employment or promotional goals. Zero.

To be fair to the PCEEO, at least in the beginning of its life, it was not really set-up to handle complaints from federal employees. It was established to address employment discrimination in the ranks of government contractors such as Lockheed and did a poor job of that. It was terribly underfunded and understaffed. Its value to the 21ers was that it allowed them to get the problems at Mare Island on the radar screen of discrimination, at Mare Island and beyond.

***

In order to formalize the complaint team, two years after the complaint was filed, Willie Long wrote Admiral Fahy asking for "The Original 21ers Club" to be officially entered into the base records, with, in part, the following language:

> The purposes of our organization are: 1. To elevate qualified minorities into every phase of Mare Island employment. 2. To create a better relationship between management and employees. 3. To better ac-

quaint our membership with working conditions of every occupation. (For details, see appendix 4.)

From that point on, the group was officially recognized and referred to as The Original 21ers, although 25 had actually signed the original complaint before it was filed. Although discrimination was not admitted in any correspondence from the Navy or the PCEEO, not then or ever, the document showed that some progress was being made, in that on the roster of officers for the organization, the occupation of Boston Banks, James Colbert, and Clarence Williams was listed as inspector, which none were at the time of the filing, and would likely not have become a reality without the filing of the complaint..

As things progressed, the PCEEO officials required Long to send monthly progress reports, including descriptions of any retribution. According to the men present at the meeting in 2003, after the complaint was filed some of them heard negative comments from other workers when they walked into a shop, but the government made it clear they were not to be touched and that there were to be no reprisals. As far as it is known, there were no direct reprisals.

Through all of this, the men stuck together, at least in the early years, continued to meet and attempted to recruit new complainants. It was not easy, because, aside from the initial attempts at "negotiations," one of the first moves at Mare Island was to continue the attempt to divide and conquer, the classic Machiavellian approach. According to Long, management tried to bribe and isolate him from the others by offering him an early promotion. He would have no part of it. "They tried to buy me off," but, he countered, "if you are going to send me up [for promotion], what about the other 24?"[16]

***

By this point and even earlier, something important had happened. Although the complainants had not gotten The Shipyard or the PCEEO to find and admit discrimination, they had, at least, gotten their attention and gotten them to listen. As such, some progress on promotions was slowly being made by 1963, but there were still many long-standing hurdles to overcome. One of the issues in the original complaint was that African Americans were not getting mis-assigned [selected for special training]. This was important, because the men who received the special mis-assignment training were the ones who most likely would be promoted to supervisor. In fact, this was especially important, because, until the late 50s, there were no exams required to be promoted, according to Jim Davis. If the shop heads liked you, according to Davis, for whatever reason, they 'blessed" you and you were promoted. In some shops, that tradition was carried on well after the 21er complaint was filed. "They would just bless you," said Davis. "Get your paperwork together and you're going to be a supervisor," a "blessed" one would be told.[17]

For the most part, the men that were interviewed by Sloan in 2003 felt that the shop heads were totally opposed to the demands that were made in the complaint. All of those interviewed felt that the shop heads were in denial and would only admit that a few mistakes had been made but not that their shops had deliberately discriminated against African Americans. In reality, the discrimination was everywhere, all around, for anyone looking to see. A good example was Eddie Brady's shop. Brady said,

> Finally, I told Wally Clark, the head man, I said, when I pass by this office, I see no black as a planner, no black in your office period. Then, he wanted to talk to me. He said he had an open door, anytime he walked through this door. So, he did offer me up there. Some of the shop heads claimed that Negroes did not get promoted because they did not attend social activities like picnics or softball games in Napa.[18]

In those days, Napa was not a welcoming town for African Americans and, in fact, many of the white shipyard workers were believed to have moved there to escape from the relatively large number of African Americans living in Vallejo.

***

For a rather significant period after the complaint was filed, even when they were given promotions, the men were often not treated the same as their white co-workers. After being promoted to planner, Boston Banks was put in a back room by himself, away from the other planners and called an analyst. He took no part in work assignments, materials purchasing, or the other things that, normally, real planners did. According to him, to show his dislike, he would sit among the plans and go to sleep. Somehow, he then came up on the list for consideration for promotion to floor supervisor, after he was asked if he would accept it. This was sometime in 1963 or 1964. According to Banks, the whole, established promotion process was difficult to navigate and people had to be diligent and persistent. To do so, Banks claimed that,

> They made [promoted] everybody on the [eligibility] list except me to supervisor in Shop 31. I never got a supervisor's job, so I went in and talked to my head of shop and told him I was going to file a complaint and I had made the preparations, I was definitely going to sign the complaint. Then...I went through the same thing. They made all the fellows on the list below me, and when I put in for a foreman or a quarterman, they made all the fellows on that list, except me, as a general foreman. So I said, look here, you want me to file a complaint on this, too? No, no, no, he came back [and] he said, well we'll find out what you can do. And, a day later, they made me a general foreman.[19]

They made him a general foreman but not in Shop 31, the shop of his choice, where he had served his apprenticeship. According to him, the leadership did not like him in Shop 31. So, instead of Shop 31, they assigned him to Shop 31E, the electrical shop, which, for some reason, was considered less prestigious. Eventually, he wound up in shop 36, the Ordinance Maintenance Shop, where he served as general foreman until he retired. What he had learned again was that "if you did not complain or not raise hell with them, they would skip right on over you."[20] It was still a struggle, even after all the complaints that were put in. "You had to go to them and tell them, look, I'm going to go do this and I'm going to file a complaint before they would [do anything]. Every time, they would have some kind of excuse."[21]

Not very long after the complaint was filed, Jim Davis was promoted to snapper in Shop 56, then, later, assigned to the Planning Department and, eventually, was promoted to Advanced Planning Manager of the Nuclear Section, a prestigious job that he would not have gotten in the past, not under any circumstances.

However, these promotions and others were part of a long process and the men still living in 2003 believed that part of the reason was that the information about the complaint and the federal response did not filter down, with

the leadership at Mare Island keeping the situation at the higher levels for discussion. Every shop head was brought into the discussions, as was John Chamberlin, Sr., a Caucasian from the Department of Industrial Relations, who,
according to Banks, "gave us more insight into what was happening than anyone."[22] Beyond that, not even all the Quartermen knew about it, and definitely
not the men at the lower levels, at least not for a long time after the federal response. "We were meeting and talking with these guys up here [at the main
administrative offices of Mare Island] but it never, it never filtered out to The
Shipyard [at large]. They [the workers] never knew a damn thing about it, according to Jim Davis."[23] This thinking is in line with what Honsinger had written in early 1962:

> After my negotiations with the group on January 17th, I personally
> discussed the problem with Heads of Departments and offices, Group
> Masters, Heads of Shops, and top people. ...I urged cooperation in
> passing the word on to the subordinates regarding the policy of the
> president and the Navy Department on Equal Employment Oppor-
> tunity. I've asked the Industrial Relations Officer to take immediate ac-
> tion regarding techniques on the part of those personnel of the
> Employment Division who deal with the public as well as Shipyard
> employees. Action is also being taken to encourage first line supervi-
> sors to consider this subject in the selection of employees for addition-
> al pay assignments, training, and details.[24]

However, in all of this, there was no direct mention of racial discrimination.
The closest to it is Honsinger's written statement that his approach would..."do
much toward eliminating the circumstances which have nurtured the feelings
of frustration which are apparent in the employees concerned in this case."[25]

In the 2003 interview, the surviving men said that, even though there was
no official or announced finding of discrimination, the leadership at Mare Island knew that something was amiss, that something was wrong, and so they
started looking at the overall promotion process itself. In the opinion of Matt
Barnes, "they started looking at such things as career ladders and the process of
how to get people from the position of helper to mechanic, the whole promotion process."[26] (This may have led to Sloan being promoted to limited mechanic in a time frame that was, for an African American, relatively, much, much

faster than it would have been in the past, probably due to the influence of younger leaders like Hank Dever and Bud Lemke). This urge to look at the process, starting at the lower levels, was very much encouraged by the filing of the complaint, some of the men felt. When Clarence Williams was asked about his experience in promotions after the complaint was filed, he said it had been fairly positive but with some hiccups. For example:

> Once I got into inspection, fortunate for me, my department head became my best friend, so that really made the working experience good for me. The highest position I had was branch head of the structural department. Actually, I turned that down after a year. I think Ed [his supervisor and patron] had retired by then. They wouldn't pay me the same salary that they paid the other department heads. When I complained about that, their answer…they had me up at a big meeting there…their suggestion to me was, just, just think about the 'prestige'. Man, prestige lived at 772 South 52nd street [his home address]. I requested to be transferred back into Refueling Department and remained there until I retired.[27]

Eddie Brady went on to become a foreman in Shop 31 and eventually became head of a training school on Mare Island. Until his death in 2009, he firmly believed that his promotions were the result of the activism of the 21ers' actions.

In the case of Jim Davis, there was not to be a happy ending at all. He, like some others, felt that the discrimination never really went away; it just changed forms. Many years later, Davis would feel that he was discriminated against in a way that the men would never have dreamed of in the beginning. In that connection, Davis related the following:

> Well, at the end my career at the shipyard, I was almost back where I filed my first complaint, because they gave a woman a promotion that I should have gotten. And so, I bought my way out. I said, well, you know, I told them that I was 58 or 59 years old and they said I could stay until I'm 70 or longer and I'll never retire. So, [I said] I'll go out if you guys give me $30,000, I said, cuz, I said, it equates to my level of what I'm applying for the next 10 or 12 years and I have basically not considered working over 80 (laughing).[28]

It was a situation that was hard for Davis to accept, because he felt that he had done all the right things. Before making his deal, he went so far as to hire an attorney to help press his case, because, at that time of the incident, he felt that he was one of the most highly trained people on Mare Island. He had received extensive training in his field from the time he was first assigned to inspection. According to him, because the shipyard leadership wanted to "show" an African American, he was sent for training that was usually reserved for shop and division heads. Over the years, he had been sent for training to such prestigious schools as Stanford University and the University of Southern California, attending various kinds of seminars and workshops related to his work. At the time that he filed his complaint, he produced documents of all his training but was told that it was old education. "That's what he said. I said, well what is old education? You know, well you have that....I assume that that you graduated from some college, is that still applicable?"[29] Of course, that conversation went nowhere.

Although Davis got some support from the leadership in his group, including his immediate supervisor, he was worn down after all the hassles over the years and, finally, gave up and made the deal to retire with a buy-out. In some ways, he would regret not staying and fighting it through, but the shipyard closed in three years anyway, and so he felt that he had not lost anything, except at the emotional level, which, with the cumulative, negative psychological impact, could not have been a good thing.

Some of the men, Boston Banks, for example, had the experience of white men not wanting to work for them and who actually refused to work for them, especially the ones from the South. However, according to Barnes and Williams, some of them eventually came around and told them that the experience had changed and improved their lives.

However, there was inevitably some resentment, some still lingering today. One Caucasian person, who worked in the same shop as Banks, today believes that "some [African Americans] got promotions that they did not deserve."[30] Another Caucasian man who worked in the shop with Banks refused to talk about the 21ers and their impact at all. Here, it should be noted that these responses probably should not be surprising. It must be understood that such attitudes are probably a reflection of what Oliver and Shapiro have identified as demonstrating, in some ways, how whites may come to develop a psychological and material stake in the social and economic arrangements that continue to marginalize and stigmatize people of color.[31] It should also be remembered that there were still many whites working at Mare Island who came from or were descendants of people from the South. Underlying much of the problem, many in leadership roles came with the belief that African Americans should be happy just to have a job and, more than likely, believed that they were in the right place in the hierarchy of rank and pay. This was clearly demonstrated in the treatment of Williams, as described above. The idea that African Americans should be paid less for equal work and responsibility was a holdover from viewing and accepting such a reality in the South. It should also be noted that some African Americans from the South found that practice to be acceptable, a fact that, ironically, had sometimes posed a great challenge to the organizing efforts of the 21ers, both before and after the filing of the complaint.

In the beginning, the group had no white supporters but, over time, they did have some. Some gave undercover support. "John Chamberlain was one of those that actually helped us get information out of the employment office that we normally wouldn't have been able to get," said Boston Banks.[32]

Some of the people the 21ers had to deal with were more difficult than others. Admiral Fahy, who was recognized by everyone for being "hard-nosed," once "came up and bumped his stomach up against me (and said), go ahead...call me a son of a bitch, called me everything else, call me a son of a bitch," claims Banks, who responded, "Admiral, if you want to be a son of bitch, you can be one, but I don't have to call you [one]."[33] This must have been an amusing sight, because Banks was a very big man and Fahy was a rather small man.

**

And so, the struggle went on, with Willie Long always in the lead, at least in the beginning. And he was relentless, always in the face of the leaders on Mare Island or writing letters to Washington, DC, and, at least in the first few years, he was supported by the other men in his approach. However, over time, some of the 21ers began to feel that he was not the right person to continue to lead the group. Eventually, with Long's hard-driving ways, things probably had to come to a head. Some of the surviving 21ers remembered him quitting his position as leader of the 21ers, but James Davis says:

> No, no, no, he was voted off, because I commented that Willie would still be president [of the 21ers] or still would have been on the shipyard, if we, cuz he'd become an embarrassment. Let's, let's, let's tell it like it is, because he was losing his cool at the meetings and sometimes you'd [Banks] be pulling his coat tail, to sit him down. Now, this is the thing. We felt, hey, we had progressed so far that we no longer needed his type of pushing. [It was felt that] he was a detriment to the organization and that broke the man's heart.[34]

Sloan remembers that Long had told him that attorney Wilson could control him and that, sometimes, he needed to be controlled. When Sloan related that comment to the group during the 2003 interview and asked Banks what was his interpretation of why the split came about, Banks responded, "I talked with Willie about what I felt we were getting done, but Willie wanted it all at once. He, he wanted all 21 [25] of those fellows that signed that complaint to move up at once. And he wanted all blacks promoted at once, to move up, and that was what caused the split."[35]

At the outset, many, if not most of the 21ers, had been opposed to the idea of every one of them simply getting an automatic promotion. At one early meeting, the question was sarcastically raised by Admiral Honsinger, the idea of simply giving everyone a promotion. The response from the original set of complainants was that they did not want to be promoted unless they were qualified. Of course, not all were qualified. Sloan, for example, had only been a helper for a little more than a year when the complaint was filed and, at the time, was not thought of as a great worker. In any case, "We said, no, we want to be qualified for it cause we were qualified," said Davis. Later, there were some second thoughts. "The white boys were getting promoted and they weren't qualified for shit, but, yet, pride, pride killed us and that was the first or second meeting we had. That slowed everything down for about 18 years, you know. That, that, our pride, our pride got in our way, when they threw that out at us."[36]

Those issues aside, any assessment of the importance and effectiveness of the 21ers has to begin with Willie Long. Although many thought they were ready to do something, more than likely nothing would have actually happened without him taking an aggressive lead, at least not in the short run. He was relentless and brought a new way of thinking to the struggle for equality at Mare Island. In line with the thinking of some of the civil rights activists at the time, he encouraged the men to move toward the approach of direct confrontation, using all the legal and other vehicles at hand. This was often difficult, because many, if not most, of the men working on The Shipyard, had migrated from the South in the 1940s and 1950s and were adverse to confrontation with a white power structure. Long, who did not want to wait any longer, probably believed to look to the future for answers is to deny your power to fully express now in the midst of racism. On the other hand, some, like Brodie Taylor, did not believe that they were confrontational enough. Be that as it may, Willie Long was very confrontational. Driven by his anger at the situation facing African Americans, he could be very abrupt and aggressive but "the attorney [Wilson] kept me pretty straight."[37] Long was angry. According to his wife, Joyce, "My husband was angry most of the time [and]...that, being mistreated like that, he had to let somebody know."[38] Long's children also saw it. "Everyone in that whole town [Madera, California] was afraid of my father," according to his daughter, Susia.[39]

Like all the other 21ers, Clarence Williams, who went on to relatively good success at Mare Island, had great respect for Willie Long:

> Willie Long was a guy that,..., lots of heart, he was committed and he always talked about what the Original 21ers were trying to do. To me, because I didn't really know John Edmondson that well, it was Willie Long and Charlie Fluker who were the two that impressed me the most. Willie Long, every time you saw him, he was always talking about the 21ers, its goals and aspirations.[40]

Later, in another interview, when asked if he had any regrets for joining with Long and the others, Williams' response was: "No. I wish we had done it even sooner."[41]

Matt Barnes held similar feelings about Willie Long. According to him, "I guess the driving thing that really got the 21ers going was...Willie Long...in his persistence. He was probably the most persistent fellow in pulling, pulling us together and trying to see that we were, could take advantage of promotions and get integrated into the other areas of the shops."[42]

Willie Long was definitely the driving force and he had no regrets about taking action. As to the older guys taking the lead, Long, in talking with Sloan in 1980, said that "If we, the older people, had taken a more secure stand, we would have made it easier for the younger people as you came along."[43]

After he was voted out as president of the 21ers, and facing his increasing disillusionment, Long left Mare Island employment and Bay Area and then moved to Madera, in the California Central Valley, to become a plumbing contractor and small scale real estate investor. He was disillusioned and some believe he was hurt and broken-hearted. The writer is among them, although believing that is often the way things go in this world. At that time, Boston Banks became the second official president of the 21ers. After that, Long only attended one of the 21er meetings, events or reunions that took place over the years after he left Mare Island. After 1964, Sloan did not see Long again until 1980 and then, unfortunately, never again. With or without the 21er connection, the fire and quest for justice remained, however. He carried his fire to Madera. Years later, when one of his daughters, now Susia Cayasso, complained that no African Americans were selected to be a cheer leader at Madera High School, Long went to the school leadership and, miraculously, an African American girl became a cheerleader.

When Long died, his wife and one daughter, Susia, believed it was at least partially from the effects of the "poisons" that were part of the environment of working on the ships and submarines. His skin had started to peel by the time of his death. In the end, his wife said that she understood what drove him: "Willie Long was Willie Long. You get tired of it. What did he have to lose? You take the time and try to straighten something out for the next generation."[44] That is what he did. Long died in 1992, a great man largely forgotten. This writer had and continues to have tremendous respect for Long and still will, sometimes, shed a quiet tear when thinking of him, his bravery, his struggles, and his sacrifices in attempting to right some glaring wrongs.

Notes:

1. *Vallejo Times Herald*, November 12, 2006, p. A3.
2. Barbara Davis email to Jake Sloan, April 9, 2014.
3. Bruce Christensen email to Jake Sloan, February 6, 2014.
4. Memo from Mare Island Commander to Bureau of Ships (BUSHIPS) March 15, 1961.
5. Memo from Mare Island Commander to BUSHIPS March 17, 1962.
6. Memo from Mare Island Commander to BUSHIPS March 15, 1962
7. Navy letter to Willie Long, June, 1962, writer unknown.
8. Ibid.
9. Admiral Fahy memo, February, 1963.
10. Edgar Dillion Letter to Mare Island Shipyard Commander, August, 1962.
11. Clarence Williams interview.
12. Banks, Barnes, *et al* interview.
13. Letter to Willie Long from John Hope II, March, 1963.
14. *Mare Island Grapevine,* October 11, 1963
15. Ibid, January 11, 1963
16. Willie Long, interview..
17. Banks, Davis, interview.
18. Banks, Barnes *et al* interview.
19. Banks, Davis interview.
20. Ibid.
21. Ibid.
22. Banks, Barnes, *et al* interview.
23. Ibid.
24. Memo from Mare Island Commander to BUSHIPS March 15, 1962
25. Ibid.
26. Banks, Barnes, *et al* interview.
27. Clarence Williams interview.
28. Banks, Davis interview.
29. Ibid.
30. John Chamberlin email to Jake Sloan, July 26, 2014

31. Melvin L Oliver and Thomas M. Shapiro. *Black Wealth/White Wealth: A New Perspective on Racial Inequality.* (New York: Rutledge Taylor and Francis Group), 2006.
32. Banks, Barnes, *et al* interview.
33. Banks, Davis interview.
34. Banks, Barnes, *et al* interview.
35. Ibid.
36. Ibid.
37. Willie Long interview
38. Joyce Long, in recorded interview by Jake Sloan. April 16, 2007. Sacramento, California.
39. Ibid.
40. Clarence Williams interview.
41. Ibid.
42. Matthew Barnes, in recorded interview by Jake Sloan. June 23, 2004, Richmond, California.
43. Willie Long interview.
44. Joyce Long interview.

CHAPTER 5

Follow up:
The Long-Term
Impacts

After the filing of the complaint, as time went on, some of the original 21ers became disenchanted with the lack of affirmative motivation on issues of discrimination on the part of many of the younger African American workers that were beginning to work at Mare Island in the ensuing decades. Banks said, "you couldn't motivate them to apply [for membership]. You couldn't motivate them to apply when they did get there."[1]

After the complaint was filed, many of the 21ers, still led by Long, at least in the beginning, had continued efforts at the recruitment of additional members. Essentially, to a great extent, they faced the same resistance they had encountered in the beginning, even though not much was asked, according to Matt Barnes:

> Join and support the goals and objectives. The goals and objectives were...to try to eliminate those things we had set out in the initial kind of complaint we made. And all of those things were applicable at that time. If you realized we were in that kind of situation and wanted to do something about it, you could become a member of the 21ers and we could do it together.[2]

Although the membership grew, somewhat, over the years after the filing of the complaint, the participation at the regular meetings was relatively small, never over 50 people and usually many fewer. Speaking further on the issue, Banks said that:

> They would support us with their name on the roll. Other than that, we got no support [from] them. I talked my head off to people and I gained nothing by talking to them. Even the people that I worked [supervised], helping them, pulled [them] up in the shop. They would not come to our meetings. However, they did pay their $2 a year membership fee [but] they would not come out and speak their voice on anything.[3]

However, a significant early addition to the team was Vernon Taylor, a distant relative of Sloan, who, like the others, had been born in the South, in Carthage, Arkansas. He would later become recognized as an honorary member of the Original 21-25, along with John Edmondson. Taylor joined soon after the complaint was filed and participated in some of the investigational testimonies. His reputation as a mechanic and as a man was impeccable. He had completed his apprenticeship in 1961. Possibly as a result of his association with the 21ers, he received some exceptional training opportunities, but was given the runaround in his aspiration to get a position in the Planning and Engineering Department, causing him to leave employment at Mare Island. In 1966, he was the first African American to be accepted as a member of Local 159 of the Plumbers/Steamfitters union, which was then located in Richmond.

***

It took time, but over the months and years following the filing of the complaint, all of the leadership of the Original 21ers, except Willie Long and Charles Fluker, received rather significant promotions and opportunities for advanced training. Although he was eventually detailed to the Design Division, John Edmondson never got a promotion to supervisor. When John retired, he took a job as a technician at Napa State Hospital, possibly to help make ends meet. He died in 1979, a great man largely forgotten, except by his family, his church and lodge members, and those who knew, worked with and respected him at Mare Island.

Some of the promotions for African Americans were very significant. However, ironically, over the years, some of the best promotions went to African Americans who had refused to sign the complaint. According to the incomparable Willie Capers,

> They was afraid of losing their job. I said, you came here, you came here looking for a job. If something help you, well, why not go ahead and fight for something that's going to benefit you. I know quite a few of them backed off, but when the day went down and things started happening, blacks started getting supervisor rates, they [were] most of the first guys that got it, compared to guys in the 21ers.[4]

It must be remembered that fear of losing a job working at the yard was understandable. Since professional opportunities were limited to non-existent, working at places like the Mare Island and Hunters Point shipyards was seen to be an opportunity for "good" jobs and stable income. The current mayor of Vallejo, an attorney, Osby Davis, worked at Mare Island as a young man, as did George Livingston, before becoming mayor of Richmond. Dewitt C. Burris, the father of famed Oakland civil rights attorney John Burris, worked in Shop 72 at Mare Island over a long period, establishing a solid economic base for his family. John's father faced the same dilemma as many African Americans working at Mare Island. According to John, "...he [Dewitt] talked about it but he held his peace, because of the need to take care of his six kids."[5] A job in the shipyard provided some stability and could prove to be a major stepping stone for an African American family to move into the middle class, which DeWitt Burris' family did over time. Probably without completely understanding the drive, people like Dewitt Burris, Clarence Williams, Matt Barnes and others were looking for the opportunity to create wealth and move into, and remain in, the solid middle class as opposed to just earning an income adequate to live on. Said Matt Barnes, "We were trying to make a better life for ourselves."[6]

Over the years, the impact of the 21ers actions was felt far beyond the workers at Mare Island. For example, the group was invited to join the Council for Civic Unity[7] and held one seat on its board. The writer and other members of the 21ers believe and there is the possibility that the actions of the 21ers influenced the passage of Title VII of the Civil Rights Act of 1964. One of the people who influenced the writing of the Act was Hobart Taylor, who served as assistant to vice president Lyndon Johnson on the PCEEO and took testimony from Willie Long and Boston Banks, among many others, at a hearing in Los Angeles sometime in late 1962 or early 1963. (However, research by the writer of Mr. Taylor's papers at the Bentley Historical Library at the University of Michigan found no specific mention of either the 21ers or Willie Long). In any case, the action definitely helped to lead to the establishment of rather strong equal employment opportunity programs at Mare Island, an effort in which Matt Barnes was actively and prominently involved. Over time, the organizers of the Original 21er group were urged to help organize African Americans at other governmental facilities. "And eventually, before the group [The 21ers] kind of faded away, we had people at Port Chicago [in Concord, California] and some of the kind of outlying facilities that expressed interest in becoming part of the group," according to Matt Barnes.[8]

As they indicated In the 2003 interview, all of the surviving members believed that if the complaint had not been filed, nothing would have changed, especially in the short run. To the question of how much influence the action of the 21ers had beyond Mare Island, Clarence Williams said that African Americans "were having the same problems at other installations, they were having the same problems that we had. At Hunters Point [Naval Shipyard in San Francisco], they wanted to know what did we [the 21rs] do."[9] The movement also spread to other federal installations, resulting in many opportunities for African American men and women throughout the Bay Area. One concrete result was the formation of Black American Federal Employees for Equal Opportunity (BAFEEO), which was a direct offspring and would eventually have a membership of more than two hundred, including some of the 21ers. BAFEEO did not survive but it was one of the forerunners of the formation of Blacks in Government, which became a national organization.

Beyond the original signers, two people are great examples of the long-term benefits of being associated with the 21ers. One example is Walter Allen. He was not an Original 21er, because he was not working on Mare Island at the time the complaint was filed, but joined later, became a devout member, and remained connected with the other members until he died in 2016. He began at Mare Island in Shop 56 as pipefitter helper in 1965. With the support of Hank

Dever, who years before had supported Sloan, he advanced in his career to become Production and Test Support Branch Head in Code 365.l. This was the non-nuclear Ship Work Control Center (SWCC), which did recertifying of submarines ready to return to sea. An important event in Walter's career took place on June 21, 1988, when he was presented an Equal Opportunity Award, which he believes was the first for an Afro-American to receive at Mare Island. The award was presented by the Shipyard Commander. After a great career at The Shipyard, Walter Allen retired in August 1994 with 34 years actual service, including time spent in the military.

The experience and success of Walter Allen is a clear example of the impact of the long-range strategy of the 21ers, which was to open opportunities for African Americans who came after them. According to Allen, "I am a product of the 21ers." Soon after he came to The Shipyard, he joined the 21ers and took on men like Boston Banks, James Davis and Clarence Williams as mentors and, without them, he claims, "I would not have known what to do," in dealing with the ongoing problems of discrimination on The Yard.[10]

Another great example of success is Willie Preston. Although he did not sign the complaint, he later became a member of the 21ers and probably reaped great benefits over time. Without the 21ers efforts, it might have taken him longer, but Preston seemed destined to move up the ladder one way or another. From a highly respected and ambitious family in North Richmond, and an athlete like Davis, Preston had started in 1953 as a helper at Mare Island in Shop 11. According to his account, after only two years, he was promoted to journeyman mechanic without first serving as a limited mechanic. In 1967, he was promoted to supervisor, then to General Foreman in 1974 and then to Shop Superintendent in 1983. He was the first black person to hold the position of Shop Superintendent in the history of the shipyard. He says that, in 1961, no one recruited him to sign the complaint. That could very well be true; not all African Americans were recruited, for various reasons, as noted above. In any case, the 21er actions could not have hurt his chances for promotion.

Notes:

1. Banks, Davis interview.
2. Banks, Barnes *et al* interview.
3. Ibid.
4. Ibid.
5. John Burris email to Jake Sloan, July 26, 2016
6. Boston, Barnes *et al* interview.
7. In 1944, a San Francisco Council for Civic Unity had been formed, made up of 400 representatives of religious, labor, business and government groups to, in the words of its president, Harold Boyd, "do something" about the city's growing racial problems. This was to be done while working with minority groups. The Pittsburg Press, October 22, 1944.
8. Banks, Barnes *et al* interview.
9. Ibid.
10. Walter Allen, in telephone interview with Jake Sloan, January 15, 2016.

CHAPTER 6

Recognition

Gradually, over time, at least partially as a result of the efforts of the 21ers, there was a period of ongoing promotions and the opening of wider opportunities for young African Americans who came to work at Mare Island. However, to a great extent, general knowledge of the 21ers and their contributions increasingly faded with time. When The Shipyard was closed in 1996, the surviving men who were still working there went into retirement, some taking other jobs to supplement their retirement incomes, and then, for the most part, their contributions to an important part of history were largely forgotten. That is, Willie Long, the other 21ers, John Edmondson, and Vernon Taylor were almost completely forgotten to history.

That reality would change in rather dramatic fashion. In November 2006, at the urging of Anthony Gilmore, Clarence Williams' nephew, who had become aware of the complaint and its aftermath, some of the surviving members of the Original 21ers met with Mathias Gafni of the *Vallejo Times Herald* to revisit memories of actions surrounding the filing of their complaint of discrimination against Mare Island. Present at the meeting were Matt Barnes, Boston Banks, Willie Capers, James Davis and Clarence Williams. The meeting took place at the comfortable, well appointed, middle class home of Matt Barnes in Richmond. As a result of that meeting, forty-five years after the filing of the complaint, the 21ers began to become recognized in a series of articles that appeared in the *Vallejo Times-Herald*.

Once the recognition started, after a series of articles in the November editions of the *Vallejo Times-Herald*, it kept rolling in. On January 4, 2007,

Congressman George Miller read a tribute into the Congressional Record and then later that month presented the tribute to the men at Touro University on Mare Island on January 18, during a celebration of its 9th Annual Tribute to Dr. Martin Luther King, Jr & Humanitarian Award Presentation. (See Appendix 5.) The presentation was part of a ceremony that also included the presentation of a Certificate of Recognition from then Vallejo Mayor Anthony J. Intintoli, Jr. On February 21, 2007, the group was recognized in a resolution by the California State Assembly, sponsored by state senator Noreen Evans and Don Perata, then President of the Assembly. Later that month, there was a well-attended roundtable discussion held at the Vallejo Naval and Historical Museum. The discussion was moderated by *Vallejo Times-Herald* reporter Mathias Gafni, the man who had originally "broken" the story. Original 21ers participating were Boston Banks, Matt Barnes, Eddie Brady, Willie Capers, James Davis, Jake Sloan and Clarence Williams. On June 9, 2016, James Davis, Louis Greer, Jake Sloan, and Clarence Williams, the surviving 21ers, were honored with the "Living History Award" by Touro University. In their wildest dreams, the men could not have begun to envision such recognition in 1961 or at any time over the years since the filing of the complaint.

A little more than 3 years after the initial recognition, what was possibly the high point of recognition came on November 17, 2010, exactly 49 years after the filing of the complaint, when a memorial stone for The 21ers was placed in historic Alden Park, across from Shop 56, where Willie Long and John Edmondson, along with several other 21ers, had worked.

Sometime in early 2007, Eddie Brady had casually mentioned to Sloan that there should be a statue or something honoring Willie Long somewhere on Mare Island. Having already thought about it, Sloan agreed and took it upon himself to make something happen, not only in recognition of Long but all the men who had stood beside and behind him. Sloan immediately started to think about ways to get a memorial placed somewhere on The Shipyard. The process would prove to be long and drawn out.

To make the project a reality, there were many large and small challenges to overcome in getting a monument placed somewhere on Mare Island. For this effort, Sloan would be greatly assisted, and sometimes led, by one of his business associates, Kitty Creech, and his wife, Mary, along with too many others to be named. Some of the larger challenges involved a decision on where it would be placed and then getting the various permits to do so. Ultimately, a decision was made to seek permits to have it placed in Alden Park, named after Commodore James Alden, who, like Farragut, had a long naval career and served during the Civil War. Then began the tedious and long drawn-out process of applying for and receiving the permits that were required, both from the developer, Lennar Mare Island, with which the city of Vallejo had contracted in 1998 to develop parts of Mare Island, and various city agencies. They included the city Planning Department and Building Departments. The Mare Island Heritage Trust and the Vallejo Architectural Heritage Foundation also had to approve the project. In addition, an encroachment permit was required. This process required the development and submittal of detailed plans and specifications for the monument. Then, there were the steps leading up to the actual fabrication of the monument, including selection of materials. After consultation with and input from all the surviving members, Sloan drafted the inscription for the stone. In addition to a narrative, the names of all the original signers were to be inscribed, along with the names of John Edmondson and Vernon Taylor, who would be recognized as honorary members. Although neither Edmondson nor Taylor signed the complaint they were both important contributors, either indirectly or directly. Upon the suggestion of Sloan, the decision to make them honorary members was approved by all the surviving 21ers. Because of cost and timing considerations, a decision was made to have the stone cast in China.

This process started in 2008. After all the approvals were received, the stone was completed and shipped first to Tennessee and then to California. By then, another year and a half had passed. Then, the process of planning the ceremony and the unveiling of the stone began. This effort included working with the Mare Island Museum, which is part of the Mare Island Historic Park Foundation, for the purpose of seating during both the planned ceremony and the buffet lunch to take place afterwards in the Museum.[1] Finally, there was the challenge of developing and mailing the program and invitations to people, 21ers and others, who had scattered far and wide, hither and yon, in the many years since the historical complaint had been filed and the closing of The Shipyard a decade and a half before. The cost related to all of this was shared by some of the surviving 21ers.

On November 17, 2010, eighty-three people assembled in historic Alden Park to pay their respects to the brotherhood that had come together almost 50 years before. Present were family members of the 21ers, friends and other supporters and well-wishers, including people associated with the Mare Island Museum and the Mare Island Historic Park Foundation. A large contingent of members of the Willie Long family was present. Surviving members of the 21ers present that day were Boston Banks, Matt Barnes, Willie Capers, James Davis, Jake Sloan, and Clarence Williams, along with Vernon Taylor, an honorary member. Walter Allen was also present. John Edmondson's daughter, Catherine Edmondson-Fulcher, was in the audience, beaming proudly.

The master of ceremonies for the emotional event was Jake Sloan. Eloquent, emotional speeches were made by Matt Barnes and Clarence Williams, Original 21ers, and by a granddaughter of Willie Long. "I had no idea his life was so influential to so many people," said Doctor Michelle Long, in speaking of Willie Long.[2] The youngest and almost certainly the least significant of the group, Sloan strongly believes, and said, in his closing remarks to the crowd, that it was not his destiny to be a leader but that it was his destiny to live long enough, gain the skills, and build the capacity and network to help to assure that the leaders, the other members, and the movement were remembered by history. Over time, that had become his primary role as a member of the brotherhood. Pushing to have this memorial stone placed was just one part of that effort. He also believes that, although he was one of the least influential and active members of all the men involved, he probably benefited more than most, if not all, of the 21ers, because of the influence that some of the men in the group would have over many of the decisions that he was to make over the next several decades. As he said that day, "Today, I am proud to be here to represent some of the greatest men that I have ever known. Since that time in the early 1960s, I have had the opportunity to meet many great men and women, but, as a group, these are the greatest men that I have ever known, bar none."[3] Jake had always looked upon it as an honor to be allowed to join and be part of such a great brotherhood.

Notes:

1. It was perfectly fitting that part of the ceremony and celebration was to take place in the Museum. The Museum is housed in historic Building 46, which housed Shop 56, where some of the 21ers often spent part of their daily working hours. Today, a display recognizing the 21ers holds a rather prominent position in the Museum. Today, many sites related to African American civil rights history are being lost. We in the local African American community are fortunate to have the display in the museum and the monument in Alden Park to commemorate the actions of the Original 21ers.

2. *Vallejo Times Herald*, November 18, 2006, p.A2.

3. Jake Sloan, 21ers memorial ceremony remarks, November 17, 2010.

Rear: Matthias Gafni, Anthony Gilmore, Jake Sloan, Clarence Williams, James Davis. **Front:** Boston Banks, Jr., John Hines, Willie Capers, Matthew Barnes, Eddie Brady. Vallejo Naval and Historical Museum. February, 2007.

Jake Sloan, Louis Greer, Boston Banks, Jr., Matthew Barnes, Willie Capers, James Davis, Clarence Williams. Holding Resolution of California Assembly, February 21, 2007

James Davis, Matthew Barnes, Eddie Brady, Jake Sloan, Boston Banks, Jr., Clarence Williams. across from Alden Park, Mare Island, November, 2006

James Davis, Clarence Williams, Louis Greer, Jake Sloan,
At Touro University Award ceremony, Mare Island June 9, 2016

CHAPTER 7

CONCLUSION/EPILOGUE

What happened at Mare Island Naval Shipyard in the early 1960s was not the result of an isolated idea, not something that happened in a vacuum. The filing of the complaint and the ensuing events was, at once, part of the unfolding of and a reflection of societal events taking place in the Bay Area and beyond at the time. At least one impact of the filing would be that prevailing attitudes and practices would forever be burst asunder at Mare Island, despite the fact that there was never an official finding of racial discrimination in hiring training, promotions and equal pay on the part of the leadership at the Shipyard. Also, the African American workers at Mare Island were part of the spearhead of the emerging new African American middle class that was, at least partially, being created by government policy. Furthermore, these African American workers/leaders were able to take advantage of and influence it, even if only indirectly. The 21ers were part of what possibly pushed the process along, helping to influence and create legislation that led to the Civil Rights Act, the Equal Employment Opportunity Commission, the War on Poverty and the associated jobs and opportunities that would be created, thus benefiting the rising professional class of African Americans, supported by such workers as the 21ers. These efforts benefited people like Doctor Michelle Long, granddaughter of Willie Long, who spoke at the unveiling of the memorial stone. They were pushing for the affirmative action for African Americans that was, at least partially, comparable to the affirmative action and privileges for whites that had been in place for so long and, to a great extent, remain intact today.

There was a great, probably unforeseen, outcome. With all the frustrations and challenges the original group faced and endured, working together caused the men to develop great respect for each other and, for the rest of their lives, they addressed each other as "mister" on all occasions. For many, if not all of the 21ers, it was their first experience of African Americans working together for a common cause, a cause that resulted in a mostly positive outcome. For many, it would be the only such experience. As Clarence Williams says, to paraphrase, in so many ways there was a certain self-respect in forging a lasting brotherhood. For Sloan, it, along with his military experience, would be a large part of the base for his general outlook and everything he did over the next several decades. The men formed a lasting bond. According to Jim Davis, in an opinion that he expressed to those present in the 2003 interview, "Well, what I got out of this is that the men, I feel, we formed a bond out of what we went through that it's hard for anyone, except who went through it, to understand it. I know, I have the utmost respect for...you guys and the people who went through it. It was a love affair."[1] All the men present at the interview agreed. In a different interview, Williams went on to say,

> I was close to the 21ers, because they helped me to advance myself, not only monetarily, but it helped me internally, mentally, and I was able to retire before I was overworked; I was not relegated to doing the heavy, manual labor. We were able to do other things. We were able to go into managerial type jobs...they [the 21ers] were directly responsible for that and I have always felt that I owe them, even though I was part of it.[2]

Without the efforts of the 21ers, some of the African American men who started working at Mare Island as apprentices probably never would have gone above being a journeyman; some of those who started as helpers never would have gone above being helpers or, at best, limited journeymen. After the 21ers action, some African Americans, including some of those who would not sign the complaint, became leading men, quartermen and even reached higher ranks. Louis Greer called some of those men "apple catchers," because they chose to not shake the tree, but caught the apples when they fell off after others shook it. What bothered some of the men was that some of the African Americans who refused to commit were given some of the best promotions. According to Willie Capers, again speaking on the subject, "When I left Mare Island...I heard about all these guys getting promoted, going up the ladder, ...and I was so enthused, but then [they were some of] the guys that didn't, didn't do nothing. They wouldn', they didn't help with nothing."[3] However, like all the others, Jake Sloan believes that "... I think it's something to be extremely proud of...that there was a group of guys, no matter how small it was, that was willing to stand up for what was right, for themselves and for others."[4]

It was a great team. Over time, however, the differences in personalities and approaches began to develop splits in the organization, as most prominently demonstrated by the departure of Willie Long from the group and from Mare Island. No matter. In the end, they all thought it was a worthy fight. With a feeling shared by many, according to Sloan, "What I was really fighting against with the 21ers, and later in life, was unfairness. The 21ers did not fight to socialize with whites; we fought to get equal employment opportunities, promotions and higher pay, fairness, in a word."[5]

Since at least the time that John Edmondson had started at Mare Island in 1930, there had been a tension between those African Americans who wanted to force change and those who wanted to settle for the status quo. Eddie Brady, like many others, believed that things would have never changed on the Island if it had not been for the actions of the 21ers. Matt Barnes thought that things would have changed but "I don't think it would have changed as much."[6] Sloan believes that things would have gradually changed as men like Hank Dever and Bud Lemke in Shop 56 moved up the ladder of leadership and responsibility.

In the final analysis, then, the 21ers group did not bring new ideas or complaints to the fore. The ongoing frustrations and complaints at Mare Island were simply crystalized under the leadership of the great Willie Long. Then, Long, and those who stood tall with him, forced change that is still being felt today. Probably wisely at the time, in the face of lack of support from other African Americans, John Edmondson had backed off on frontal confrontation, although he continued to be critical of what obtained at Mare Island. Long would not back-off. Ever. To paraphrase Paulo Freire, "Freedom is acquired by conquest, not by gift. It must be pursued constantly and responsibly."[7] Such is the case with equality of opportunity, which was pursued constantly and responsibly by Long and his followers. There is little if any doubt that the action took nerve. Says Jim Kern, curator of the Vallejo Naval and Historical Museum, "I think it's a big deal, just trying to buck the military hierarchy. The military is very ingrained. It took a lot of guts to stand up to that. You have to give them a lot of credit."[8] Many are indebted to Long and the other 21ers, whether knowingly or not. Some semblance of equality, self-determination and empowerment was made possible by the efforts of several but speeded up by Willie Long, who stood tall, very tall.

***

When this writer again thought seriously about undertaking the writing of this work, in 2003, there were eight survivors from the 25 who signed the complaint in 1961. At this writing, all but four of the Original 25 are deceased. James Davis, 82, is living in retirement at his home in Vallejo; Louis Greer, still active and working at 95, is owner of a jewelry and watch repair store and an investor, living in Berkeley; Jake Sloan, 76, is owner of a labor-management consulting firm headquartered in Oakland, and lives in Richmond; Clarence Williams, 82, is living in retirement at his home in Richmond. All are comfortable. They meet from time to time. Vernon Taylor, 82, an honorary member, lives in retirement in Las Vegas. He stays in contact with Davis and Sloan. Still standing tall, and proud of what they did, they are the surviving members of a great brotherhood, formed a long time ago in a hostile environment.

Notes:
1.   Banks, Barnes et al interview.
2.   Clarence Williams interview.
3.   Banks, Barnes et al interview.
4.   Ibid.
5.   Jake Sloan, Foundations. Op. Cit.
6.   Barnes interview.
7.   Paulo Freire, Pedagogy of the Oppressed. (New York: Continuum, 1993), p. 31.
8.   Vallejo Times Herald, November 18, 2006. P. A3

RESEARCH METHODOLOGY AND SOURCES

For many reasons, the research for writing of this book was carried out over almost 40 years; some of it began even before I started working on this effort. However, it has always been all connected to my commitment to influencing and recording social change and justice in the construction and building trades, in particular, and in the general society of the San Francisco/Oakland Bay Area. With great support from others, the basis of my research methodology for this particular effort has been to make every attempt to understand the events that took place in the early 1960s and retold here, all in the context of that time, but taken with a long view. I have attempted to make the approach to research as participatory as possible, to the extent that I often effectively played the role of a participant in some of the interviews that I conducted, and to the extent that I actively solicited the recollections of those who were heavily involved at the time.

The research for this work was made difficult and greatly influenced by two major factors. First, a lot of time had elapsed before the serious research began. As such, much time had passed before I interviewed any of the participants in the events, with the exception of Willie Long, whom I interviewed in 1980. As a result, of course, much had been forgotten. Secondly, especially when I first started, for my part, there was an almost complete lack of access to real-time documentation, either in the hands of the surviving 21ers or others. There were other challenging factors, but these were the hardest to overcome. To the extent that the work was in any way easy was due to the fact that I had been a participant in some of the early stage events, which gave me immediate and complete access to the surviving players when I started, as well as some ideas about what to ask them. With all that in mind, I used the following methodology and approach to the research, documentation and writing, with great support from many.

INTERVIEWS AND CONVERSATIONS:

Interviews were a fundamental component of the research. In conducting, and sometimes participating in the interviews, I wanted the work to go beyond what was already in print or rumored and get to the real story, based on first-hand experience, and so I strove to make the approach and process participatory, and one that reflected as wide an angle of observation and viewpoints as possible. To the extent possible, I wanted to interface with the people who were directly involved, the 21ers themselves, and people who were only one or two stages removed, which included family members, friends, co-workers and professionals. I also wanted to get input from those who did not approve of the actions taken by the 21ers. For that process to proceed logically, in my mind, my interview with Willie Long was a major driver for the fundamental research required in developing the work. It basically started there, because he was the most formidable of the key players in the events that unfolded in the making of the story. That interview took place only 19 years after the filing of the complaint, which means that, relatively speaking, his memory was fresher than those interviewed twenty to thirty or more years later.

After reviewing the Willie Long 1980 interview, I interviewed all of the other seven 21ers who were alive in 2003. I took the position that I was part of the interviews and helped to answer some the questions that I posed. To proceed, first I interviewed a larger group that did not include Louis Greer. I then interviewed all the survivors individually, including Greer. In some cases, over a number of years after 2003, I interviewed surviving 21ers more than once, either individually or in groups. I did so because the men represented several different production shops, and each shop at Mare Island operated a little differently than the others, along with the fact that some shops were more racist in their views toward African Americans than others. The follow up interviews with the individuals were also important, because I really wanted to get beneath the surface, which meant probing what the players brought to the table from their regional upbringing and training. For some reason, Boston Banks and James Davis wanted to be interviewed together. That was interesting, because after Long left they were probably the two most powerful players in the group. Above all, I wanted to get at what the people were thinking at the time, although we were decades removed from the events. The interviews with the 21ers were very instructive, because one of my challenges was the fact that I was only 21 years old at the time of the filing of the complaint and eventually only worked at Mare Island for a little more than four years. As such, my knowledge of the shipyard and its operations was not deep at all. Even some of what I had once known had been forgotten. As such, as the work progressed, I had to rethink some things, based on what I learned from the ongoing interviews, the documentation aand the general story of the history of the period, For example, the book *John Grider's Century: African Americans in Solano, Napa and Sonoma Counties from 1845 to 1925,*opened my eyes to the period of the early 20th century in Vallejo, Solano County and The Shipyard, which led me to a better understanding of people like John Edmondson and how he had responded to the changing attitudes brought on by large numbers of Southern born or influenced Caucasians coming to work at The Shipyard in the 1930s and, especially, the 1940s.

The interviews with the 21ers were instructive and enlightening at more than one level. For example, it did not bother me that the comments from some of the 21ers were not always grammatically correct, although I noticed them. I knew the men well and they were extremely articulate in conveying their thoughts and emotions, with the possible exception of Capers. Even with him, I understood him, and I knew that he knew what he was talking about and that he was honest to a fault. It helped that I am fluent in their idiom/patois, having spent my first years in the backwoods of Arkansas. I grew up with people who talked the same way, including my father, who was one of the smartest men that I have known. I also knew that Capers had grown up in rural Louisiana, where the chance for most African Americans to get a good basic education was remote at best, and sometimes, verging on impossible when he was growing up.

Everything related the process of preparing for and executing the interviews, especially as time passed, all helped me in putting some things in historical perspective, a perspective that I was sorely lacking at the beginning of the process.

After my initial interviews with the surviving 21ers, I began to interview some of their surviving relatives. First, I interviewed the widow of Willie Long and one of his daughters. To conduct the interview, I first had to locate Mrs. Long, finding her in Sacramento, California. In 2007, I interviewed her and a daughter, Susia Cayasso, in Susia's home in Sacramento. This interview was very instructive in understanding the background and outlook of Willie Long, as well as the impact of his actions on his family, which supplemented what I knew from direct experience and my discussions with Jim Davis and the other 21ers. It also gave me some insight into Willie Long's relationships with some of the other men who would become 21ers, as well as his relationship with John Edmondson, along with additional ideas for follow up interviews. In that connection, as further described below, I interviewed Catherine Edmondson-Fulcher, the daughter of John Edmondson, the man who had such a profound influence over Willie Long, in particular, but also over many other African American and non-African American workers at Mare Island.

In order to get a feel for what drove attorney Charles Wilson, the legal and political counsel for the 21ers, I interviewed his widow and a daughter, and read contemporary news accounts of his actions in local newspapers, actions such as running for a seat on the Berkeley School Board, which were given to me during the interview. His actions, especially his active involvement in the NAACP, and the East Bay Democratic Club, coupled with his support of the 21er effort at modest retainer, at best, indicated an impressive and deep commitment to the advancement of African Americans.

What struck me most during the interviews with relatives was the fact that none of them, with the possible exception of the wife of Clarence Williams, knew much of anything about the filing of the complaint or follow up actions except what they had read beginning in 2006. If fact, Mrs. Williams, who participated in one of my interviews with her husband, was the only relative whom I interviewed during any of my direct interviews with the surviving 21ers. I think this was another proof of the overriding concern for secrecy as the events had unfolded back in the early 1960s.

I also interviewed people who were not directly connected to the 21ers, but benefitted from their actions, people such as Novena Hunt, whose husband worked in Shop 56 in the years after the complaint was filed.

I interviewed as many people as possible who lived during that time and who were familiar with the players and surrounding events, as well as the general social, political and economic realities of the time. For example, I interviewed Joyce Giles and Barbara Davis, volunteers who work at the Mare Island Museum. Both are Caucasian. Ms. Giles worked at Mare Island before its closure, including administrative work related to EEO compliance. Her husband worked in Shop 31 with Boston Banks. Both were very helpful, in the interviews, in assisting in my research at the Museum, and later in volunteering to review a draft of this work.

In addition to in-person interviews, I conducted some by phone or email. Sometimes after face to face interviews, I conducted follow up calls to people such as Walter Allen, who had joined the 21ers when he started employment at Mare Island in the mid-1960s after Long had left. I exchanged emails with Bruce Christensen, a Caucasian, who worked at Mare Island from 1957 until its closure in 1996. Mr. Christensen's father worked at Mare Island with Matt Barnes, one of the original 21ers. He was very helpful in explaining how the shipyard was organized. Mr. John Chamberlin worked at Mare Island in the same shop as Boston Banks. His father also worked at Mare Island and was helpful to the 21ers in their efforts to gain valuable information from the personnel office. I quoted both in the work above. I thought it was important to get the views of non-African Americans, both from those who were supportive and no-supportive, as shown in interviews cited in the body of the work above. I had met both of them in the course of getting approvals for the placement of the memorial stone, and so I had already developed some rapport with them before I undertook the interviews. They were both very helpful, because they were working at Mare Island during the unfolding of the events and because they could, as I did, benefit from looking at things from an historical, more detached perspective. Their knowledge of shipyard operations was invaluable.

To get help from the academic side, I had conversations with Professor Robert Cherny, who was one of the advisors for my MA Thesis, which was based on the subject of discrimination in the building trades, and was accepted in December of 1979 by the History Department at San Francisco State University. Professor Cherny also read a draft of the work, and gave me very helpful comments on content and structure. A draft was read by Michael McAvoy of the Western Institute of Social Research (WISR), which was followed by face-to-face discussions as the work progressed. Vera Labat of WISR also reviewed and commented on a draft. A draft was read by Leonard McNeal, a long-time friend and colleague who worked in the building trades as an ironworker and later became an adjunct professor in political science at Contra Costa College.

The final draft before completion for publication was reviewed by professor John Logan, Director of Labor and Employment Studies at San Francisco State University, and by Sharon McGriff-Payne, the author of *John Grider's Century: African Americans in Solano, Napa and Sonoma Counties from 1845 to 1925*. From the beginning and throughout the course of completing the work, I sought the advice and counsel of Doctor John Bilorusky, President, and Marilyn Jackson, a faculty member at WISR.

After a the next-to-last draft of the work was completed, it was reviewed by James Davis, Vernon Taylor, and Clarence Williams, all 21ers. Taylor not only read it but had his daughter, an educator, to review and comment. Interviews and conversations followed the reviews, including a group meeting to discuss the progress of the work.

READINGS

In addition to the interviews, and in order to get a better, more general feel for the times and the influences on Long, the other 21ers, and the other African American workers, I read a rather wide-range of books reflecting life and society in the 1950s and 1960s. These readings included works on labor history, civil rights history, biographies, autobiographies, general histories and economic history. Here, I will identify some but not all of the books that were reviewed.

In order to get some feel for African American life in Vallejo and Sonoma County in the 20th century, I read *John Grider's Century: African Americans in Solano, Napa and Sonoma Counties from 1845 to 1925,*by Sharon McGriff Payne, which was very instructive on the social, political, and economic relations between whites and African Americans, both in Vallejo and on Mare Island, as well as the general life of African Americans in Sonoma County.

A relatively large number of the men who became 21ers lived in Richmond. Beyond interviews and personal recollections, in order to get a feel for their daily lives and influences, I read *To Place These Deeds: The African American Community in Richmond, California, 1910-1963*, by Shirley Ann Wilson-Moore, an African American professor of history at Sacramento State University.

To research African American activism in Oakland in the 1940s and 1950s, where Willie Long, and several others who became 21ers lived, I read *American Babylon* by Robert O. Self. To get a feeling for the changing times and a different kind of rising activism beginning in the 1960s, I read *Revolutionary Suicide* by Huey P. Newton, a founder and leader of the Black Panther Party in the 1960s and 1970s.

For an understanding of the political realities that obtained at the national level, I read several books. For a general understanding of the John F. Kennedy administration, I read *A Thousand Days: John F. Kennedy in the White House*, by Arthur M. Schlesinger. For an understanding on Kennedy's specific views on African Americans and civil rights, I read *Bystander: John F. Kennedy and the Struggle for Black Equality*, by Nick Bryant. For an understanding of other views, I read Robert A. Caro's *The Years of Lyndon Johnson: The passage of Power*, a detailed look at the vice presidency of Johnson and his role in civil rights at the time. For a more conservative angle, I read *Goldwater* by Barry Goldwater and Jack Casserly. For a look into the insider roles of African Americans in the Kennedy and Johnson administrations, I read *Walking with Presidents: Louis Martin and the Rise of Black Political Power*. This is the story of an outstanding African American who had influence in the administrations of both Kennedy and Johnson in the 1960s. I also read general and biographical documents on Hobart Taylor, Jr., who was general counsel to the PCEE0.

To get an understanding of the thinking of both whites and African Americans about such things as tiered or unequal wages, I read *Slavery by Another Name* by Douglass Blackmon and *The Negro Worker* by Ray Marshall.

To get some feel for and an understanding of the inferiority complexes displayed by some, if not most, African Americans at the time, including the workers on Mare Island, I read the works of E. Franklin Frazier and Franz Fanon, specifically, *Black Bourgeoisie* and *Black Skin, White Masks,* respectively.

To better understand the general history of Mare Island I read *Closure: The Final Twenty Years of MARE ISLAND NAVAL SHIPYARD* and *Sidewheelers to Nuclear Power: A Pictorial Essay Covering 123 Years at Mare Island Shipyard,* both by Sue Lemmon and *The Long Line of Ships* by Arnold S. Lott.

In some cases, especially in working on the relationship of African Americans to the Building Trades unions, I resorted to work that I had done years ago in wring a thesis for an MA degree in history. *Blacks in Construction: A Case Study of Oakland, California, and the Oakland Public Schools Construction Program 1960-1978* in some ways dealt with the same subject a couple of decades after the 21er complaints, but with a longer historical development and a focus on the problem in the non-governmental work of the building and construction trades unions.

Of course, I read all the game-changing articles on the 21ers prepared by Mathias Gafni for *The Vallejo Times-Herald,* published in 2006 and 2007. They were invaluable in getting me started, but they did not go deep enough, did not get to the underlying feelings and driving forces of either the complainants or their adversaries. With that in mind, I developed a set of interview questions to get at those challenges, to the extent possible, with a special focus on questions that I would ask in interviews of family members.

LIBRARIES AND ARCHIVES

For some of the research, I had to go to special libraries and archives. For example, because of what I had been told by some of the 21ers, I thought there had been a meeting in Los Angeles between Willie Long and Boston Banks with Hobart Taylor, who was the special counsel to the PCEEO and a confidant of Lyndon Johnson. I wanted to verify that connection, because I thought that could prove a rather direct connection with the Civil Rights Act of 1964, over which Taylor had some influence. For this effort, I traveled to the University of Michigan in Ann Arbor to do research at the Bentley Historical Library. To my regret, I found no mention of the 21ers, Willie Long, or Boston Banks in Taylor's papers archived there.

I was fortunate that Mathias Gafni had gathered some documents from Naval Archives and Records Administration (NARA) in San Bruno, California, which I used extensively in investigating the official responses to the complaint. This was an invaluable resource that made the work much stronger. I had attempted to do research there, but had difficulty with how it was organized, which is to say, haphazardly, at best.

At the Mare Island Museum, I reviewed copies of the *Mare Island Grapevine*, the official newsletter for The Shipyard, for various periods from 1945 to 1964, and the *Vallejo Times Herald*.. (There is now a display on the 21ers at the museum that connects some of the activities to the tragedy at Port Chicago). The museum is housed in historic Building 46, which housed Shop 56 until The Shipyard was closed in 1996.

OTHER:

The belated recognition of the 21ers led to unexpected discoveries. For example, a workshop/panel discussion at the Vallejo Naval and Historical

Museum, with participation from a large audience with a range of people, including former employees at Mare Island, resulted in a large turnout. After the panel discussion, the rather large audience offered facts and ideas that had not occurred to me, which were helpful in preparing for future interviews. For example, there were Hispanics in the audience who talked about the impact the 21ers had on their employment and promotion opportunities and their relations with supervisors. It also provided the opportunity for a chance meeting with the daughter of John Edmondson, who was in the audience that day. This led to an interview that was very instructive in understanding the background and outlook of Edmondson, which supplemented what I knew from direct experience and my discussions with Willie Long and James Davis. She has lived her whole life in Vallejo and her experience enhanced my understanding of the social and political relations between whites and African Americans. Interestingly enough, it turned out that, until I made a passing comment about it, she was totally unaware that her father had influenced the 21ers.

Since so much time had elapsed since I had actually worked on Mare Island and over the many years as I worked on this effort, I sometimes casually walked or drove around The Shipyard, in an attempt to feel the ghosts of times past and the people who had worked there. As I walked or drove, some things came back to me. At the same time, sometimes spurred by the interviews and sometimes by my thoughts from the past, I began keeping a diary/memoire bank, possibly to be read by my children and grandchildren, but also to further spur my memory on important things that happened so many years ago.

***

With the opportunity to do it again, what would I do differently? After thinking a lot about the question, the answer is nothing. First of all, if I had followed up right away after the interview with Willie Long in 1980, which was the first thought that came to mind, I would have missed many important developments. The full story had not unfolded. Far from it. For example, there is no way that I could have predicted how James Davis' career ended at Mare Island, which is an important part of the full story. The story would not have gotten the same recognition that it got from Mathias Gafni's articles in the *Vallejo-Times Herald* if it had been written in the 1980s. There would have been no recognition in the Congressional record if I had written the story in the 1980s, because we would not have had the connections to make it happen, even if we had thought of it, which I doubt. Many of the books that I read to round-out my thinking were not published until after the 1980s. In the 1980s, I could not have afforded to fly to Michigan to do the research on Hobart Taylor. Not all the material and non-material pieces that I needed to do justice to the story were in place or readily accessible to me until relatively recently. The more I think about it, the more I believe that, at this particular time, and the necessary resources, allowed me to do the proper research to tell the story the best that I could. I only wish that all the Original 21ers were alive to benefit from reading the result of the research and writing, and to see the monument dedicated to them in beautiful Alden Park.

Memorial Unveiling Ceremony
The Original 21/25

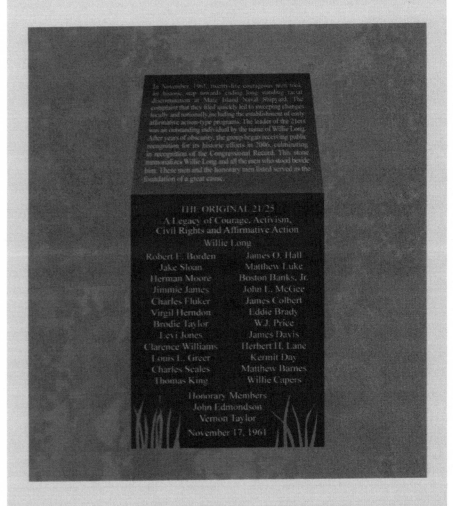

November 17, 2010
11:OO AM

Appendix 1
Mare Island Naval Shipyard Organization —1960

Shipyard Commander Admiral/Captain (USN) Code 100

Planning Officer Captain (USN) Code 200	Production Officer Captain (USN) Code 300	Public Works Officer Captain (USN) Code 400	Supply Officer Captain (USN) Code 500	Comptroller Captain (USN) Code 600
Head Design Division, Head Planner/Estimator, and **Head Nuclear Engineering Division**	**Shop Masters: Pipe Shop, Electric Shop, Machine Shop, Rigging Shop, Shipfitters Shop, Sheetmetal Shop, etc.**	**Shop Master:** Transportation Shop, Power Plant, etc. and **Design Division Head:** Engineering/Technical	Deputy Supply Officer Commander (USN)	Deputy Comptroller Commander (USN), Assistant Comptroller. (civilian)
Branch Head	**Shop Foreman**	Foreman/Chief Quarterman, Branch Head	Branch Head	Division Head
Supervisory Engineer, Technician, Planner and Estimator (P&E)	**Chief Quarterman /Quarterm an**	Quarterman, Supervisory Engineer. Technician, (P&E)	Leadingman/ Supervisor	Comptroller Branch Head/ Supervisor
Lead Engineer and Techician	**Leadingman (supervisor)**	Leadingman, Lead Engineer and Technician	Lead Supply Stockman	Lead Payroll and Accounting
Engineers and Technicians	**Snapper (Lead Journeyman)**	Journeyman	Warehouse Attendant, Supply Clerk, etc.	Payroll and Accounting Clerks
	Journeyman	Apprentice		
	Apprentice	Limited Mechanic		
	Limited Mechanic	Helper		

Notes: 1. Due to space limitations several Departments are not shown; e.g., Codes 120 (Industrial Control Dept), 130 (Quality Assurance), 140 (Management Info), 150 (IRO), 700 (Medical), 800 (Admin. And Security). **2.** The military (US Navy) Planning Officer, Production Officer, Public Works Officer, Supply Officer, and Comptroller all reported directly to the Shipyard Commander. Some of the civilian Managers, such as the Head of the Design Division, the Head Nuclear Engineer, and specific Shop Masters (such as Irv Whitthorne) also reported directly to the Shipyard Commander.

Appendix 2
The Original 21-25

Willie Long

Boston Banks, Jr

Jimmie James

Matthew Barnes

Levi Jones

Robert Borden

Thomas King

Eddie Brady

Herbert Lane

Willie Capers

Matthew Luke

James Colbert

John L. McGee

James Davis

Herman Moore

Kermit Day

W. J. Price

Charles Fluker

Charles Scales

Louis Greer

Jesse "Jake" Sloan

James D. Hall

Brodie Taylor

Virgil Herndon

Clarence Williams

Appendix 3, page 1

1   COMPLAINT OF RACIAL DISCRIMINATION

2   TO: PRESIDENT'S COMMITTEE ON EQUAL JOB OPPORTUNIES

3   Washington 25, D. C.

4   FROM: THE UNDERSIGNED, EMPLOYEES OF THE MARE ISLAND NAVAL SHIP-

5   YARD, VALLEJO, CALIFORNIA, THE RESPONDENT HEREIN

6

7   The complainants whose signatures appear at the end this

8   document make the following complaint against the Mare Island

9   Shipyard, Vallejo, California. We are presently employed at this

10   shipyard and have many years of service at this installation. Con-

11   ditions have reached such a sad state regarding discrimination

12   against Negroes that we are forced to appeal to your Committee

13   for some kind of redress. The following are specific circum-

14   stances and conditions that exist at this shipyard to the detri-

15   ment and harm of the Negro employees:

16   1.There is an established unwritten practice at the Mare Is-

17   land Shipyard Shipyard not to upgrade of third step mechanic no

18   matter what the qualificatins of the employee are at any given

19   time. As a result there are Negro employees with fifteen to

20   twenty years of experience still in this category while white

21   workers with much less experience and time have moved rapidly

22   up the ladder of promotion.

23

24   2. Negro employees are systematic barred supervisory posi-

25   tions although many are entitled to such positions by reason

26   of seniority and experience. There are two Negro leadingmen sand

27   blasters and one Negro leadingman laborer out of a force of hun-

28   dreds of supervisors. We have statistics to prove that several

29   Negroes are qualified for some of these supervisory jobs but are

30   prevented by devious methods of disqualification.

31   3. Negroes who take examinations for advancement are for the

32   most part flunked on the oral interview. This is board made u

Appendix 3, page 2

of three top supervisors within the shop. As long as this situation exists Negroes will never be able to advance through examination.

4. Young Negro men are refused the opportunity for apprenticeship training for the most part. In shop No. 56 no Negro apprentices have been hired in the last three years. Those who have passed through the apprenticeship program have the best chance of qualifying for supervisory positions so in denying Negroes equal opportunity in the apprenticeship program he is also being denied the equal opportunity at the supervisory positions.

5. In over twenty years at Mare Island no Negro mechanic has ever received a Superior Accomplishment Award to our knowledge. This is often a monetary award for some superior workmanship in the shop and out on the ship. Many of the white employees have received such awards but not the Negro employees.

6. In the new field of Atomic Shipbuilding at the shipyard men had to be trained and are still being trained for certain new positions. There are no Negroes who have been selected for training in this new program. This is racial discrimination.

7. Negroes are discriminated against in the post apprenticeship training programs. Negroes as a general practice are not given credit for training related to their jobs that they take on their own in order to advance themselves. In fact Negroes are discouraged from takeing any training by management. White employees are not treated in this fashion.

8. White employees are given the easier and preferred jobs while Negroes are given the hard and unpopular jobs. For example, in shop 71 all of the spray painters in the spray booth are white even though there are many Negroes qualified

Appendix 3, page 3

to do this job. There are Negro sandblasters who are denied
overtime on week ends but white employees are given this overtime work.

been
9. There are some paint helpers who have/helpers for fifteen to sixteen years and have not been promoted to painter.

We therefore respectfully request that your committee investigate and correct the deplorable conditions as outlined above.
Any communication addressed to this group should be mailed to:

> Mr. Willie Long
> 341 Bergedo Drive
> Oakland, California

Respectfully yours,

[Signatures]

Dated: Nov. 17, 1961

Appendix 3, page 4

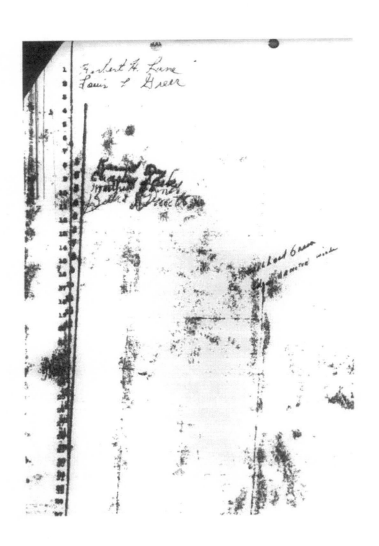

Appendix 4

8 November 1963

Rear Admiral Edward J. Fahy
Commander
Mare Island Naval Shipyard
Vallejo, California

Dear Sir:

This letter is submitted as a request that the identity of our group be entered in the records of the Shipyard's Industrial Relations Office under the provisions of NCPI 721.6.

The name of our organization is: The Original 21ers Club, a branch of the Bay Area Federal Employees for Equal Opportunity (MISS Unit).

The purposes of our organization are:

1. To elevate qualified minorities into every phase of Mare Island employment.

2. To create a better relationship between management and employees.

3. To better acquaint our membership with working conditions of every occupation.

The following is a current roster of officers of our organization:

President	Willie Long, Shop 56
Vice President	Boston Banks, Inspector
Rec. Secretary	Clarence Williams, Inspector
Corres. Secretary	Charles Scales, Shop 56
Sgt. At Arms	Eddie I. Brady, Shop 31
Treasurer	James Colbert, Inspector
Parliamentarian	Matthew Barnes, Shop 36

In order to become a member one must be of good character, willing to abide by the laws of the organization, employed at Mare Island Naval Shipyard, willing to meet the financial obligations, and willing to attend regular meetings.

The organization is open to prospective members regardless of race, creed or color.

Our membership requests a meeting of representatives of The Original 21ers Club with you at an early date. Purpose of the meeting is to discuss matters of mutual interest and to give consideration to the establishment of regularly scheduled meetings of our representatives with the Shipyard Commander.

Sincerely yours,

WILLIE LONG
President

Appendix 5

Congressional Record

PROCEEDINGS AND DEBATES OF THE *109th* CONGRESS, SECOND SESSION

United States of America

House of Representatives

TRIBUTE TO MARE ISLAND ORIGINAL 21ERS

--

SPEECH OF
HON. GEORGE MILLER
OF CALIFORNIA
IN THE HOUSE OF REPRESENTATIVES
THURSDAY, JANUARY 4, 2006

Mr. GEORGE MILLER of California. Madam Speaker, I rise today to invite my colleagues to join me in honoring the Mare Island Original 21ers for their efforts to end racial discrimination at Mare Island Naval Shipyard.

On Nov. 17, 1962, twenty-one African American workers at Mare Island Naval Shipyard in Vallejo, CA, took a historic step by filing a racial discrimination complaint with President Kennedy's newly created Committee on Equal Job Opportunities. The complaint quickly helped lead to sweeping changes locally at the shipyard and nationally at military installations, including early Affirmative Action-type programs. All the men wanted was a wage comparable to their white co-workers and to be treated equally. What they started was a chain reaction that reverberated around the country. The group would become known as the Mare Island Original 21ers, and would forever change the base's social landscape.

Despite these pioneering steps, their early civil rights efforts remain in obscurity. The group's surviving members still talk about the movement, but the full story was buried in the 1960s and only recently came to light as a result of a series of newspaper articles by Vallejo Times Herald reporter Matthias Gafni.

Their story is typical of the time. Vallejo was a Navy town, and a separated one. With its naval shipyard, Vallejo has always had a population reflecting a wide range of ethnic backgrounds; but it was not always harmonious. In the late 1950s minorities were mostly working in unskilled positions at Mare Island as sandblasters, laborers and cleaners, with efforts to keep them out of certain positions. The discrimination was not restricted to withholding promotions and unfair hiring practices, according to one of the workers. At every phase of each work day they faced discrimination.

By 1960 the Civil Rights Movement was in its infancy and the African American workers were losing patience. In March 1961, President Kennedy issued an executive order establishing a sweeping, government-wide Equal Employment Opportunity Policy. Twenty-one workers began organizing under the leadership of Willie Long, meeting in complete secrecy to protect their safety and their jobs. A complaint was drafted and twenty-five workers ultimately signed it. The complaint covered deplorable conditions for black workers, involving promotions, the apprenticeship program, and general unfair treatment. The shipyard commander found no pattern of discrimination, but President Kennedy's committee was inundated with similar complaints from around the country and changes were finally made after several years. Almost everyone who signed the original complaint was promoted to supervisor and fortunately escaped any of the serious reprisals they feared.

Their quiet but risky fight for equal treatment helped change our Nation. These heroic men included Willie Long, Boston Banks, Jr., Matthew Barnes, Louis Greer, Jake Sloan, Charles Fluker, Clarence Williams, James Davis, Thomas King, Robert E. Borden, James O. Hall, Matthew Luke, Herman Moore, Jimmie James, John L. McGhee, James J. Colbert, Virgil N. Herndon, Eddie Brady, Brodie Taylor, W.J. Price, Levi Jones, Herbert H. Lane, Kennit Day, and Charles Scales.

Madam Speaker, in tribute to these men and their fight for equal rights, it is proper for us, and it is indeed my honor, to formally recognize the Mare Island Original 21ers, and thank them for their heroic actions.

Author's Interviews

1. Walter Allen, March 7, 2007. Vallejo, California.
2. Walter Allen by telephone. September 12, 2015
3. Boston Banks and James Davis, July 2, 2004. Vallejo, California.
4. Matthew Barnes, June 23, 2004. Richmond, California
5. Eddie Brady, March 6, 2007. Vallejo, California
6. Catherine Edmondson-Fulcher. March 5, 2007. Vallejo, California.
7. John Chamberlin. Email. July 26, 2014
8. Bruce Christensen. Email. February 3, 2014.
9. Barbara Davis and Joyce Giles. March 19, 2007. Vallejo, California (Mare Island)
10. Louis Greer, February 20, 2008. Berkeley, California
11. Noveena Hunt. March 27, 2007. Benicia, California.
12. Joyce Long. April 16, 2007. Sacramento, California.
13. Willie Long, 1980. Madera, California
14. Vernon Taylor. Email, June, 2004
15. Clarence Williams. February 25, 2007. Berkeley, California
16. Lucy Wilson. March 29, 2007. El Cerrito, California
17. Boston Banks, Matthew Barnes, Eddie Brady, Willie Capers, James Davis, Jake Sloan, Clarence Williams, March 22, 2003. Richmond, CA.
18. James Davis, Jake Sloan, Vernon Tayler, Clarence Williams. November 5, 2014. Vallejo, California

Selected Bibliography

1. Anderson, Terry H. *The Pursuit of Fairness*; A History of Affirmative Action. New York: Oxford University Press, 2004.
2. Blackmon, Douglass A. *Slavery by Another Name: The Re-Enslavement of Black Americans from the Civil War to World War II*. New York: Anchor Books, 2008.
3. Bryant, Nick. *The Bystander: John F. Kennedy and the Struggle for Black Equality*. New York: Basic Books, 2006.
4. Caro, Robert. *The years of Lyndon Johnson: The Passage of Power*. New York: Alfred A. Knop, 2012.

5.   Fanon, Franz. *Black Skin, White Masks.* New York: Grove Press, 1952.

6.   Frazier, E. Franklin. *Black Bourgeoisie.* New York: Simon & Schuster, Free Press Paperbacks, 1997.

7.   Freire, Paulo. *Pedagogy of the Oppressed.* New York: Continuum, 1993.

8.   Friedlander, Peter. *The Emergence of a UAW Local:1936-1939: A Study in Class and Culture.* Pittsburg: University of Pittsburg Press, 1975.

9.   Goldwater, Barry, with Jack Casserly. *Goldwater.* New York: Doubleday, 1988.

10. Howard-Pitney, David. *Martin Luther King, Jr., Malcolm X, and the Civil Rights Struggle of the 1950s and 1960S: A Brief history with Documents.* New York: BEDFORD/ST. MARTINS, 2004.

11. Jacobs, John. *A Rage for Justice: The Passion and Politics of Phillip Burton.* Berkeley: University of California Press, 1995.

12. Katznelson, Ira. *When Affirmative Action Was White: An Untold History of Racial Inequality in Twentieth Century America.* New York: W.W. Norton &Company, 2005.

13. Lemmon, Sue. Closure: *The Final Twenty Years of MARE ISLAND NAVAL SHIPYARD.* Vallejo: Sue Lemmon and Silverback Books, 2001.

14. Lemmon, Sue and E. D. Wichels. *Sidewheelers to Nuclear Power: A Pictorial Essay Covering 123 Years at The Mare Island Shipyard.* Hong Kong, 1977. Library of Congress Catalog No. 77-90050.

15. Lott, Arnold S. *A Long Line of Ships: Mare Island's Century of Naval Activity in California.* United States Naval Institute, 1954.

16. Mack, Kenneth W. *Representing the Race: The Creation of the Civil Rights Lawyer.* Cambridge: Harvard University Press, 2012.

17. Malcom X. *The Autobiography of Malcolm X, as told to Alex Haley.* New York: Ballantine Books, 1965.

18. McGriff-Payne, Sharon. *John Grider's Century: African Americans in Solano, Napa and Sonoma Counties from 1845 to 1925.* New York: Universe, Inc., 2009.

19. Marshal, Ray. *The Negro and Organized Labor.* New York: John Wiley & Sons, Inc., 1965.

20. Newton, Huey P. *Revolutionary Suicide.* New York: Penguin Books, 1973.

21. Obama, Barack. *The Audacity of Hope: Thoughts on Reclaiming the American Dream.* New York: Three Rivers Press, 2006.

22. Oliver, Melvin L. and Thomas M. Shapiro. *Black Wealth/White Wealth: A New Perspective on Racial Inequality.* New York: Routledge Taylor & Francis Group, 2006.
23. Peele, Thomas. *Killing the Messenger: The Story of Radical Faith, Racism's Backlash, and the Assassination of a Journalist.* New York: Crown Publishers, 2012.
24. Poinsett, Alex. *Walking with Presidents: Louis Martin and the Rise of Black Political Power.* New York: Madison Books, 1977.*
25. Richardson, James. *Willie Brown: A Biography.* Berkeley: University of California Press, 1996.
26. Robinson, Archie. *George Meany and his Times.* NY: Simon & Schuster, 1981.
27. Rowen, Richard L and Lester Rubin. *Opening the Skilled Construction Trades to Blacks: A Study of the Washington and Indianapolis Plans for Minority Employment.* Philadelphia: University of Pennsylvania, 1971.
28. Self, Robert O. *American Babylon: Race and the Struggle for Postwar Oakland.* Princeton: Princeton University Press, 2003.
29. Sheinkin, Steve. *The Port Chicago 50: Disaster. Mutiny, and the Fight for Civil Rights.* New York: Roaring Brook Press, 2014. *
30. Sloan, Jesse L "Jake." *Blacks in Construction: A Case Study of Oakland, California, and the Oakland Public Schools Construction Program 1960-1978.* Unpublished Master's Thesis. San Francisco State University, 1979. Unpublished
31. Starr, Kevin. *Golden Dreams: California in an Age of Abundance 1950-1963.* New York: Oxford University Press, 2009.
32. Tye, Larry. *Rising From the Rails: Pullman Porters and the Making of the Black Middle Class. New York:* Henry Holt and Company, 2004.
33. Weiss, Nancy J. *Whitney M. Young and the Struggle for Civil Rights.* Princeton, New Jersey: Princeton University Press, 1989.
34. Williams, Juan. *Thurgood Marshall: American Revolutionary.* New York: Times Books, 1998.
35. Wilson Moore, Shirley Ann. *To Place These Deeds. The African American Community in Richmond, California 1910-1963.* Berk: Univ of CAPress, 2000.
36. Wofford, Harris. *Of Kennedys and Kings: Making Sense of the Sixties.* Pittsburg: University of Pennsylvania Press, 1980.

About The Author

After serving in the military, Jake Sloan started his working career as a pipefitter, working mainly on the construction of nuclear submarines. After leaving that field of work, while attending college, for a number of years he worked mainly in the area of programs directed at equal access and equality in training and pay for African Americans in building trades in the San Francisco-Oakland Bay Area. Since 1985, Mr. Sloan has owned Davillier-Sloan, Inc., one of California's largest labor-management consulting firms, with a focus on the construction industry.

Mr. Sloan holds an MA degree in history from San Francisco State University. The subject of his MA thesis was *Blacks in Construction: A Case Study of Oakland, California, and the Oakland Public Schools Construction Program 1960-1978.*